SUCCESSFUL
FRANCHISING

Other Books in the Instant Success Series

The Real Estate Coach by Bradley J. Sugars
Billionaire in Training by Bradley J. Sugars
Instant Cashflow by Bradley J. Sugars
Instant Sales by Bradley J. Sugars
Instant Leads by Bradley J. Sugars
Instant Profit by Bradley J. Sugars
Instant Promotions by Bradley J. Sugars
Instant Repeat Business by Bradley J. Sugars
Instant Team Building by Bradley J. Sugars
Instant Systems by Bradley J. Sugars
Instant Referrals by Bradley J. Sugars
Instant Advertising by Bradley J. Sugars
The Business Coach by Bradley J. Sugars

SUCCESSFUL FRANCHISING

BRADLEY J. SUGARS

McGraw-Hill

New York   Chicago   San Francisco   Lisbon   London
Madrid   Mexico City   Milan   New Delhi   San Juan
Seoul   Singapore   Sydney   Toronto

2 3 4 5 6 7 8 9 0   FGR/FGR   0 9 8 7 6

ISBN 0-07-146671-1

This publication is designed to provide accurate and authoritative information in regard to the subject matter covered. It is sold with the understanding that neither the author nor the publisher is engaged in rendering legal, accounting, or other professional service. If legal advice or other expert assistance is required, the services of a competent professional person should be sought.
—From a Declaration of Principles jointly adopted by Committee of the American Bar Association and a Committee of Publishers.

McGraw-Hill books are available at special quantity discounts to use as premiums and sales promotions, or for use in corporate training programs. For more information, please write to the Director of Special Sales, McGraw-Hill Professional, Two Penn Plaza, New York, NY 10121-2298. Or contact your local bookstore.

Library of Congress Cataloging-in-Publication Data
Sugars, Bradley J.
  Successful franchising / Bradley J. Sugars.—1st ed.
     p.   cm.
  ISBN 0-07-146671-1 (alk. paper)
  1. Franchises (Retail trade)   I. Title.
  HF5429.23.S84 2006
  658.8'708—dc22   2005025345

Franchising is an exciting option that allows you to sell your business, over and over again, without losing control of the business. It is an option you could consider if you want to raise a large amount of money quickly.

Brad Sugars

■ ACKNOWLEDGMENTS

Thanks to Rich Roberts, Communications Director of the Cendant Hotel Group, and to Howard Johnson International, Inc. for details of the Howard Johnson story.

■ CONTENTS

▌ INTRODUCTION

Did you know? _____

The Subway restaurant chain was named the number-one franchise opportunity for 2005 by *Entrepreneur* magazine in its twenty-sixth annual Franchise 500 rankings.

This was the thirteenth time in the past 15 years that this prestigious honor has been awarded to Subway.

Subway is the world's largest submarine sandwich franchise, with more than 23,800 locations in 83 countries.

Subway origins began in 1965, when 17-year-old Fred DeLuca and family friend Peter Buck opened Pete's Super Submarines in Bridgeport, Connecticut. With a loan from Buck for $1000, Fred DeLuca hoped the sandwich shop would earn enough to put him through college. After struggling through the first few years, the founders changed the company's name to Subway and began franchising in 1974.

It's been said that there are many ways to fame and fortune, but as far as I can see, some are better than others. You could, for instance, become wealthy by winning the lotto, but who in their right mind would include this as a cornerstone of their financial strategy?

You could make your fortune through sports, but here again, you'd have to be very, very good at it to have any chance of realizing your financial ambition. And you'd better ensure that your chosen sport is one in which big paychecks are par for the course. Try even covering your costs by taking part in judo or hockey!

You could marry into money. This has been done more than a few times. Or you could sing for your supper. All you need is one top-10 song and you're laughing. Those that have the talent—and it is a talent—can make an extraordinary amount of money. The music industry is bulging with billionaires.

The trouble with these strategies is that they rely either on luck or a natural talent. But what if you aren't prepared to take the ultimate gamble? What if you weren't born with a natural sporting talent or a beautiful voice? What if you didn't have the creative juices to pen a catchy melody?

Well, there's always business.

That's right, business is, in my view, the surest way to wealth and riches. Once you've come to realize that being an employee will get you nowhere, you'll quickly understand what being in business can do for you. But you have to take that first step. You have to understand that, with few exceptions, the word *job* actually means *Just Over Broke*. And that's why I believe there are only two reasons for having a job: to gain knowledge and to accumulate capital. That's all. If you aren't learning anything new in your current job, or if you aren't accumulating capital to get started in business for yourself, then leave that job. It's that simple.

Hang on, I hear you say. What about investing in shares or real estate? Isn't that a way to look after your financial aspirations?

Sure they are, but in my view, they are best left until *after* you've begun making sufficient returns through business. You see, by first accumulating profit from your business and then investing that in real estate or the stock market (and preferably in that order) you'll be ensuring you don't end up like so many "financially secure" people—asset rich but cash poor! What's the point of that? Get the cash first, and then you can buy all the real estate or shares that you want.

So how do you get into business? Well, there are three proven routes.

- First, you could start one yourself. This is probably the first choice of most people who want to go it alone. But is it the best? In business today, buying customers is the most expensive purchase you'll ever make. You're paying retail when you're buying customers. Let me explain this. If you spend $1000 in advertising and get 10 new customers, then you're paying $100 ($1000/10) per new customer. Ask anyone who started a new company what the hardest part was, and by far and away, all will agree it was getting customers. Starting a business from scratch is also a huge waste of your most valuable asset—time. Think about it for a moment. Start your own business and it will take you somewhere between one and five years to become profitable. Buy an existing business that's already profitable (or just about profitable) and you've saved yourself those years. This is one very important lesson most people wish they had learned when they first started out. Someone once said to me that the biggest reason people fail in business is a lack of start-up capital. Yes, that's true, but only because they started the business themselves and had to pay retail for everything.

- The second way of getting into business is to buy one wholesale. This is generally the method I recommend. So what exactly is buying wholesale? What does it mean? Essentially what we're looking at is a whole new frame of reference about buying stuff. Most people negotiate based on the advertised price. I negotiate based on the initial price of *zero*. That's right; most people work their way down from the advertised price, whereas I negotiate from zero and have them justify why it's worth anything at all. Sure, it takes a special kind of thinking to succeed in buying businesses this way. I live by a simple negotiation mantra—"I have more persistence than you have resistance." You see, I'm willing to wait and wait and wait until a deal works, and if the deal never works, then so be it. My golden rule is this: Fall in love with the deal, not the business. One question that commonly arises when I start to mention buying a business for little or no money is, "Why would they sell it to me for so little?" Hopefully, you've already thought of a few answers. Most of the answers are emotional rather than logical: divorce, sickness, tiredness, pregnancy, travel, or just plain sick and tired of working too many hours for too little money. One final point: Buying wholesale takes discipline; it takes following up and abiding strictly by your investment rules. Anyone can go out and pay full price for a business. It takes an artist, an entrepreneur, to make a deal and have everyone leave the table happy.

- The third way of getting into business is to buy retail. What does this mean? To me you're paying retail if you buy the business for a price anywhere near the advertised price. And by anywhere near, I mean anything more than half of what they've advertised it for. With this in mind there are several reasons why I recommend you should use this purchasing method.

However, I suggest that you only ever pay retail for your first few businesses. First you need to get these first few running at a profit without your having to work in them. Then when you've got enough time and money, move on to wholesale deals. So, what are my reasons for paying the retail price? There are three:

Reason 1 At least you've got a start. The business is up and running, and making a profit. This profit is extremely important if you're paying retail. You want built-in profits that give you a planned return on investment before you even have to build the business. And, if you're paying full price, you want full profits. Make sure you get the previous owner to work with you for up to a month, as part of the purchase price, to train you. One important thing about previous owners, though, is that they're still blinded by what you can't do, based on their experience. Always be willing to try something new, even though they may feel it won't work.

Reason 2 You're about to learn a lot. While I'd recommend negotiating on the price, remember the main objective of your first business is to learn and grow, and secondly to make money and profits.

Reason 3 The most powerful time to pay retail is when you're investing in a proven franchise. Franchising has removed many of the pitfalls for the business buyer. And while many franchise systems are great, there are also many that are pitiful. Many people starting franchises do so with no idea of how to support you or how to help you to succeed. Be aware that the best franchises are generally the ones you will have to pay a solid price for. However, remember to look for profit, not turnover. One last point about buying at a retail price: while it's not the best way to buy, it's still a solid way for first-time buyers to invest in a proven system that can fast track both your profits and your learning experience.

This book is all about how to succeed in franchising. It's not about the different types of franchises that exist in the modern business world and it isn't intended to be an academic overview of this form of business. This book is all about helping *you* to navigate through the tides of franchising so you can make informed decisions about whether it is a viable option, what to ensure if you are selling a franchise, and what lies ahead if you are contemplating franchising an existing business.

This book is all about how to *succeed* in franchising.

This book is about *Action*. It is based on real experiences and real examples. It contains powerful information that you can put to use *right now*.

And perhaps more importantly, this book is simple to understand. It is based on knowledge that I have acquired over the years. And it's tested knowledge that I have used myself for great personal reward.

This knowledge has been distilled, so it's easy to understand and use right away. So please, consider this book your personal coach. I will be imparting *invaluable* knowledge about how to get on the fast track to profitability through franchising.

■ THE *ACTION* STORY:
TURNING DREAMS INTO REALITY

Did you know? _____

Action International is the world's first business-to-business sales and marketing coaching firm.

When *Action* opened its doors for business, it was operated out of the back room of a suburban home in Brisbane, Australia.

Today *Action* operates out of more than 700 offices in 20 countries, including Australia, New Zealand, Asia, Canada, Mexico, Europe, the United Kingdom, and the United States.

_____

At this point, you might be asking yourself what qualifies me to write a book about how to succeed in franchising. And that's a fair question.

Let me tell you.

I believe I know a few things about succeeding in this industry because I've learned the hard way. I've built my company, *Action International*, up from nothing to being ranked as the nineteeth Fastest Growing Franchise in the world, and ranked 123rd in the Top 500 by the U.S.A.'s *Entrepreneur* magazine. And this has been achieved in just eight years!

Sure I've made mistakes along the way. After all, that's what learning is all about. But there's another important qualification I have for writing this book. I have studied how to succeed in franchising, because my business is all about coaching other businesses to succeed at what they do. You could say I have a vested interest in success.

And the systems I developed have successfully taken many businesses down the franchise path.

My story isn't unique. Many others have realized their dreams just as I have.

But it does go to show that you can achieve whatever you want if you're focused and committed. You need to have a vision, and you need to think big. Then you need to get into action. And it doesn't really matter how young or old you are. I started my first business when I was 15, and Colonel Harland Sanders of KFC fame was 65 when he used his $105 Social Security check to start his business.

My story is all about turning dreams into reality. And not just my dreams, but also the dreams of the countless thousands of business owners my coaches and I have worked with over the years.

My dad decided I was going to be a businessman when he found me selling my Christmas presents to my brothers when I was only seven. The following year I'd become much smarter and worked out that if I just rented my toys to them for a day or two at a time, I got the money and the toys back afterwards.

I'm so glad now that I was a different kind of child, one who was so interested in business and money rather than just getting a job.

There is another thing that others may think of as a sin, but I now see as a virtue. I am *unemployable*. I found this out when I was 15 and tried to have a part-time job, not realizing that thinking for myself and outshining my boss wouldn't do me any favors.

It's been a long road since then, owning many businesses of all shapes and sizes, being awarded an accounting degree, making a lot of money, losing a lot of money, investing a lot of money, traveling the globe several times over, teaching hundreds of thousands of businesspeople, writing several best-selling books and building a worldwide conglomerate. Also, living a great life with amazing relationships with my family, friends, and business colleagues.

It all began, I guess, when, as a 15-year-old boy, I employed my friends as paper delivery boys and gleaned a few dollars for the papers they delivered. Since then my businesses have become a little more sophisticated, yet still based on the same principle, which is finding something people want to buy, and selling it to them, making sure I have charged well and given great service.

By the time I'd finished University, I had completed a Bachelor of Business in Accounting and worked in 27 different jobs, ranging from gardener to pipe maker, from pizza cook to radio announcer, and from disc jockey to accounts clerk. And do you want to know the one thing this experience had taught me? It was this: very few people ever gave anything their best.

As soon as I'd left college, I got a sales job and invested every single dollar I earned into training myself. Courses on money, investing, sales, business, personal growth. You name it; I did a course in it. You see, I knew that to achieve what I wanted out of life wasn't going to be about how hard I worked, but about how much I knew.

By the time I was 21, I was running four retail stores and had a photocopy management contract, earning a salary of $60,000 a year.

My mom almost had a heart attack when I told her that I had quit to go and work for myself. Being young and naive was probably a good thing. I had no capital, but a lot of smart ideas on how to create sales, how to market, and how to lead a team of people.

I bought into a women's fashion store with no money down. What I offered them instead of money for my 33 percent holding was the ability to create sales.

You reckon that was foolish of them, don't you? Well, I increased sales by 93 percent over the first nine weeks and sold my interest back to the other partners just three months later.

I did the same with a pizza manufacturing business; I took their product from just being sold in cafes to having it stocked on the shelves of Woolworths, as well as almost every other small retailer in Queensland. I funded this growth with my earnings from the women's wear store.

I was, at the same time, doing some business consulting during my spare time.

It was this consulting work that really led me to where I am today. One gentleman I offered my services to *(I used to give away two hours of my time for free, just so people could understand what I could do for them)* operated an international training company. This gentleman was best-selling author Robert Kiyosaki. He asked me to come and train his seminar promoters in the art of marketing. Little did I know then what was in store.

Training 30 seminar promoters in Hawaii meant that I was bound to go into the presenting business. Seminars in Hong Kong, New Zealand, and Melbourne meant the sale of the pizza business to create an international operation training and consulting to business owners and managers. Robert asked me to conduct training sessions at his Business School for Entrepreneurs in Hawaii later that year. That was July 1994, and 350 business owners from around the world and 11 trainers (mostly in their 40s and 50s) were there to learn from me!

That was pretty heady stuff for me at the time, and it meant I would have to concentrate 100 percent of my time and effort on it if I was to complete this assignment successfully. There was only one thing to do. I had to find a business partner who could run my business affairs back home while I was presenting seminars, consulting, and basically generating cashflow.

Once that was in place, I then proceeded to present literally hundreds of seminars all over Australia, New Zealand, Asia, and the United States.

I arrived back home in January 1995 to find that, not only was I extremely tired, sick of travel, and missing the routine of regular business, but I was also actually broke.

And so I learned my very first major business lesson: partnerships don't always work.

I suddenly found myself seriously in debt—to the tune of a few million dollars! I had no option but to move back into my parents' house.

At first I was devastated. I found it difficult to get motivated and wondered what on earth I was going to do to get out of this mess. Do you want to know what the scariest thing was at the time? I almost went out and got a job. Even though I'd just spent the last 11 months teaching everyone else how to make money, I spent three full days just sitting quietly wondering why I couldn't seem to do the same for myself. At the time I thought that life could never get any worse.

Then my dad came in one day and said, "You can't just sit there moping; get out and do something to sort this out."

That was it. I suddenly had the motivation I was looking for. The first thing I did was to get a phone line connected. Then I put a desk next to my bed and started all over again.

I sent a letter to every one of my past clients, seminar attendees, and everyone else I knew, offering my consulting services once more. After a few solid days on the phone, I was back in business. I sat down and wrote out the Vision, Mission, and Culture Statement of the new company I was going to create. I had decided to stay in the business of training business owners, but this time I'd be sure to do it well.

This is what I came up with:

Action International

Business Coaching That's Guaranteed
to Improve Your Performance

The Vision You'll Support:

World Abundance through Business Re-education

The Mission Statement You'll Embody

Action International is a team of committed, positive, and successful people who are always striving to be balanced, integrated, and honest. We will work within our *"14 Points of Culture"* to make sure that everyone who touches or is touched by the *Action International* team will benefit greatly and in some way move closer to becoming the people they want to be or achieve the goals they want to achieve.

We will always work in co-opetition with all those who believe they are in competition with us.

We are in the business of edutainment. We will educate ourselves, our clients, and all those whom we work with, while we entertain them and create a fun learning environment. We will educate our clients in world-class marketing and business development techniques using audio, video, CDs, other technologies, and simple workbooks, workshops, and seminar formats.

Our products and services will be of the highest quality, value for the money, and whether sourced from within the company or externally, will always add the most value and use the latest and most effective training methodologies available.

Action International clients, whether they are small, medium, or large in size will have a desire to have us help them in achieving their goals and be able to take on our commitment to them by returning their commitment to *Action*. They will be forward thinking, willing to learn and grow, and willing to work as a team player in the development of an organization of "people."

Our clients will be selected more on attitude than size and they will want to deal with us because we understand people are important; systems should run a company; we offer the most practical, most applicable, and fastest strategies of growth; and most importantly because we mean what we say.

We will give people back their spirit and freedom through business development.

This Uniqueness Helps to Position *Action International* with ...

The World's Most Practical Marketing and Business Development because Being in Business should Give You More life.

Action's 14 Points of Culture

1. Commitment
I give myself and everything I commit to 100 percent until I succeed. I am committed to the Vision, Mission, Culture, and success of *Action International*, its current and future team, and its clients at all times. I will always recommend products and services of *Action International* prior to going outside the company.

2. Ownership
I am truly responsible for my actions and outcomes and own everything that takes place in my work and my life. I am accountable for my results and I know that for things to change, first I must change.

3. Integrity
I always speak the truth. What I promise is what I deliver. I only ever make agreements with myself and others that I am willing and intend to keep. I communicate any potential broken agreements at the first opportunity and I clear up all broken agreements immediately.

4. Excellence

Good enough isn't. I always deliver products and services of exceptional quality that add value to all involved for the long term. I look for ways to do more with less and stay on a path of constant and never-ending improvement and innovation.

5. Communication

I speak positively of my fellow team members, my clients, and *Action International* in both public and private. I speak with good purpose using empowering and positive conversation. I never use or listen to sarcasm or gossip. I acknowledge what is being said as true for the speaker at that moment and I take responsibility for responses to my communication. I greet and say good-bye to people using their names. I will always apologize for any upsets first and then look for a solution. I only ever discuss concerns in private with the person involved.

6. Success

I totally focus my thoughts, energy, and attention on the successful outcome of whatever I am doing. I am willing to win and allow others to win: Win/Win. At all times, I display my inner pride, prosperity, competence, and personal confidence. I am a successful person.

7. Education

I learn from my mistakes. I consistently learn, grow, and master so that I can help my fellow team members and clients learn, grow, and master too. I am an educator and allow my clients to make their own intelligent decisions about their future, remembering that it is their future. I impart practical and usable knowledge rather than just theory.

8. Teamwork

I am a team player and team leader. I do whatever it takes to stay together and achieve team goals. I focus on cooperation and always come to a resolution, not a compromise. I am flexible in my work and able to change if what I'm doing is not working. I ask for help when I need it and am compassionate to others who ask me.

9. Balance

I have a balanced approach to life, remembering that my spiritual, social, physical, and family aspects are just as important as my financial and intellectual. I complete my work and my most important tasks first, so I can have quality time to myself, with my family, and also to renew.

10. Fun

I view my life as a journey to be enjoyed and appreciated and I create an atmosphere of fun and happiness so all around me enjoy it as well.

11. Systems

I always look to the system for a solution. If a challenge arises I use a system correction before I look for a people correction. I use a system solution in my innovation rather than a people solution. I follow the system exactly until a new system is introduced. I suggest system improvements at my first opportunity.

12. Consistency

I am consistent in my actions so my clients and teammates can feel comfortable in dealing with me at all times. I am disciplined in my work so my results, growth, and success are consistent.

13. Gratitude

I am a truly grateful person. I say thank-you and show appreciation often and in many ways, so that all around me know how much I appreciate everything and everyone I have in my life. I celebrate my wins and the wins of my clients and team. I consistently catch myself and other people doing things right.

14. Abundance

I am an abundant person. I deserve my abundance and I am easily able to both give and receive it. I allow abundance in all areas of my life by respecting my own self-worth and that of all others. I am rewarded to the level that I create abundance for others, and I accept that abundance only shows up in my life to the level at which I show up.

In March of that year my best friend from university began working with me. We worked from my parents' "granny flat." I recorded sets of tapes while doing the seminars, kept selling and consulting during the day, and continued selling the tapes. We stayed up until about ten or eleven o'clock each night planning and systemizing. We were preparing the groundwork for a business that could be replicated time and time again. In essence, we were preparing to franchise the business.

It wasn't long before I'd paid back everything I owed, saved a few dollars, and had a plan in place to create an amazing worldwide organization. To cut a long story short, within three years and after many trials and tribulations, I managed to create a company called *Action International*. I had employed 24 people in

Australia to take care of the business in Australia and New Zealand. A joint venture deal (worth several millions of dollars) was then signed to open an office in Singapore to service Southeast Asia, and in 1998 I felt everything was in place to enable me to make the big decision to go global through franchising.

It had been a whirlwind couple of years, with over 188,000 people attending *Action* seminars, 14,300 participating in my intensive workshops, and 397 businesses benefiting from *Action* consulting services.

So what did we do to prepare the company for franchising?

I first sat down and developed a set of personal goals, which was what I called the Brad Sugars' Entrepreneur's Credo. This is what it contained:

Be organized. Schedule a written program of your activities and objectives and stick with it the entire day.

Be dedicated. Do at least one thing every day that you should have done, but have been putting off.

Be confident. Feel as good as possible and achieve a sense of well-being by meditating at least 15 minutes every day. Exercise for another 15 minutes every day.

Be appreciative. Tell your family, friends, and business associates how much you appreciate them every week. Be generous with your praise and compliments.

Be optimistic. Leave past failures in the past, and think and focus positively on your future.

Be educated. Read something that will improve your mind every day. Keep yourself away from nonproductive people, activities, and news.

Be thrifty. Never pay full price, consume less, and never pay any more tax than is absolutely necessary.

Be sociable. Be charming and agreeable; never speak badly of anyone.

Be alert. Open yourself to new ideas, experiences, and people who can teach you something new. Stay out of ruts and routines.

Be dependable. Meet all of your business, social, and moral obligations punctually, honestly, and honorably.

Be decisive. Make the decision right now.

Be human. Remember to experience the journey as well as the results.

Be tough. Demand only the highest and the best standards of everyone you surround yourself with.

Give and you shall receive.

These 14 points became the belief system that guided the way I lived through each and every day. This became my system of personal principles or beliefs. Sure it took time to replace the old set of beliefs, but by working at it slowly and focusing on each one every single day, I was soon able to adopt them so that they became my guiding light.

They became my "14 Commandments." I was amazed at how powerful they were once I began following them. And best of all, once they had become second nature to me, they actually began to make the work I was doing to establish a franchise business easier. Suddenly, things that would previously have seemed a huge challenge were tackled with ease. My team felt happier, more empowered, and assured that contributions were indeed appreciated. Outsiders picked this up too, and would comment at the unique atmosphere within our company. It was fantastic.

Encouraged by this, and with a new lease on life, I sat down and wrote a document that detailed what I called my categories and roles. This is what I committed to:

Category: Physical Body

Role: Healthy athlete and work-out king

Category: Spiritual Life

Role: Amazing, godlike being

Category: Emotional Life

Role: Creator of my own meanings, feelings, and experiences

Role: Giver of amazing experiences

Category: Friendships

Role: Fun-loving, inspirational, and reliable buddy

Category: Family

Role: Loving son and amazing, inspirational brother

Role: Supportive, loving, and exciting best friend to my partner

Category: Personal Development

Role: Growth king and super learner

Role: Seeker and creator of exciting new learning opportunities

Category: Contribution

Role: Provider to the community, founder of the Brad Sugars Trust

Category: Good Life

Role: Creator of amazingly wonderful, balancing events

Category: Financial Freedom

Role: Skilled, highly successful, wealth-producing, positive cashflow asset acquirer

Role: Super, money-managing, high-ROI-producing, tax-minimizing multimillionaire

Category: Business

Role: In-demand business presenter, educator, and amazing facilitator

Role: Supportive, intelligent, and reasonable business partner

Role: Chairman, key strategist, and presenter for *Action International* Pty Ltd

Role: Chairman, key strategist, and presenter for *Action* Australia Ltd

Role: Chairman, key strategist, and presenter for *Action International* (Asia) Pty Ltd

Role: Partner, key strategist, and trainer for Trophy Dog Food and Associated Companies

Role: Partner and key sponsorship creator for Teardrop Pty Ltd & Lifeline

Role: Chairman and key strategist for On-Hold *Action* Pty Ltd

Role: Chairman and key strategist for Co-opetition Pty Ltd

Role: Chairman and key strategist for Geoffrey Johns Group Pty Ltd

Role: Chairman and key strategist for QBN Properties Pty Ltd

Role: Chairman and key strategist for L&B Hairdressing Pty Ltd

Role: Creator of best-selling learning tools and education programs

Role: Acquisition monster, opportunity spotter, and business turnaround expert

Role: International best-selling author

Role: Highly called upon business and media personality

I had set myself clear, and challenging, goals. I had a vision. And I had stopped dreaming. You see, my dream was taking on the appearance of reality. I was actually beginning to live my dream.

My team and I then set about developing systems that were based on the tried and tested methodologies that we had used to great effect during the previous couple of years. Let's now look at some of these in greater detail.

Due to the nature of what the company does—business coaching—we would definitely fit the definition of a Business Format Franchise. What we would be selling would be a comprehensive system that our franchisees would follow to the letter to achieve results for their clients. We would be selling a system that would include absolutely everything from business planning to management tools, and from computer systems to training and backup. Consistency and uniformity were to be major hallmarks of our system.

What followed were long days and even longer nights, but we had a lot of fun. We brainstormed, developed drafts, discarded them and started again, and refined each system after testing and measuring, before finally coming up with something that we were happy with.

These are the systems we developed:

- Sales systems
- Business presentation system

- Consultant's training system
- Business Coach's system
- Marketing system
- Accounts system
- Stock ordering system

Of course, this wasn't the end of it. We wrote manuals for each system as well as key performance indicators for each and every position.

But let's get into some of the detail here. This should give you a better idea of what's involved in developing these systems.

The Business Coach's system included an Ultimate Marketing Plan. This was what it involved, from a development point of view:

- First Contact Script
- Welcome System—fax and kit
- 12-Month Goals
- 4-Day Workshop/Calendar/Booking Forms
- Progress Checklist
- Alignment Template
- Plan of *Action* (SWOT Box)
- Video/Book Schedule
- Testing And Measuring Systems
- Consultation Booking Schedule
- Client Consultation Scripts
- Client Monthly Formula
- Copywriter's Brief
- Consultation Goals
- Critique Forms
- Results Forms

- Coach Piece Check Forms

- Congratulations System

- Monthly Progress Report

- Quarterly Progress Report

- Phone Scripts

- PERT Goals

- Mission Statement

Each system contained details of every aspect of that function you could possibly imagine. You see, the secret is to write everything down in the finest of detail so that *anyone* could do that job if they were given the manual. These systems become the very lifeblood of the company. And because companies must, by their very nature, grow as time passes, the systems too evolve as circumstances change. Remember, business is like a tree; it is either growing or it is dying. Staying the same is not an option.

Our systems changed as circumstances changed. Systems need to be dynamic to succeed. And that's really the beauty of them. That way, if a problem arises in the business, you focus first on fixing the system rather than zeroing in on the hapless person. This way you avoid, to a large extent, all those nasty and destructive personnel issues that so often sour previously harmonious companies. One of our key contentions is that systems should run the company, while people run the systems.

Today when a person buys an *Action* franchise she receives everything she'll need to get into business in the quickest possible time to start generating business and cashflow. She is sent away on a comprehensive live-in training course that lasts 10 days. She also receives the following set of six manuals:

Initial Training: Getting into Your *Action* Business

Kickstart: Getting Your Business into *Action*

Marketing: Building Your Inquiry Funnel

Sales: Converting Your Inquiry

Alignment: Getting Your Clients Focused

Coaching: Building Your Client's Business

Master Licensees receive, in addition to the above list, a *Master Licensees Manual*. We also supply them with a *Business Development Manager's Manual*.

All this is backed up with a state-of-the-art Internet-based "Member's Directory," which is an online powerhouse of knowledge, business resources, communication tools, and a discussion forum.

We've come a long way in an incredibly short period of time. In just nine short years, we've spread our wings and operate out of offices in Australia, New Zealand, the United States, the United Kingdom, Ireland, Malaysia, Singapore, China, and Mexico. Our Global Head Office is in Brisbane, Australia.

And we've had our fair share of challenges along the way. Some of them were what one would expect from any rapidly expanding business, and others were more taxing—like having to go through the traumatic, and costly, exercise of changing our entire U.S. management team during 2001–2002.

My current goal is to sell 2008 franchises by the year 2008. Ambitious maybe, but so far we are on track to achieve that.

> The quality of your life is determined by the quality of the decisions you make, which is determined by the quality of questions you ask, which is determined by the quality of your education.
>
> ***Brad Sugars***

PART 1

■ Humble Beginnings—The Birth of a New Way of Doing Business

Did you know? _____

The town of Evanston, Illinois, was known as being so religious-minded in the late nineteenth century that it was nicknamed Heavenston. They passed an ordinance forbidding the sale of ice cream sodas on Sundays. Not wanting to be shortchanged or to break the law, enterprising businessmen then started serving the ice cream with syrup instead of soda. These Sunday sodas, as they became known, were so popular that people started demanding them on other days of the week as well, and not just on Sundays. The town fathers then objected to the product being named after the Sabbath, so the businessmen changed the spelling to sundae.

The simple ice cream and milk shake may have a lot to answer for. You see, not only did they evolve into some of the most quintessential of all American icons, but also they had a lot to do with the birth of a whole new way of doing business. You see, they were at the center of the evolution of a new business system that became known as franchising.

This amazing story began back in 1925 with a man named Howard Johnson.

Who was Howard Johnson? Howard Dearing Johnson was one of those rare human beings who see their destiny, and have the drive, the talent, and the imagination to seize it. He set out to make a name for himself, and didn't rest until that name had become one of the world's great brands, and one of the best-known landmarks in travel.

He not only built one of the first great restaurant chains and one of the first midprice hotel chains, but also he pioneered many of the most successful food service and hospitality innovations. The franchisee ownership concept, the turnpike restaurant concept, the super premium ice cream concept, the "theme" restaurant concept, the commissary food distribution concept, the "America's Menu" concept, the quality motor lodge concept, the "Kids-Go-Free" family travel concept—they are all classic examples of the business and marketing genius of Howard Johnson.

It's a great American success story, and it all began at a small-town soda fountain.

In 1925, Howard Johnson borrowed $2000 to buy a small corner drugstore in Wollaston, Massachusetts. It sold candy, newspapers, and patent medicine, but Howard quickly noticed that the real action was at his old marble soda fountain. He figured that if he could invent a better-tasting ice cream cone, the world (or at least Wollaston) would beat a path to the Howard Johnson store.

He came up with a "secret formula" for vanilla and chocolate ice cream. The secret was, in fact, based on his mother's recipe for ice cream—with all natural ingredients and twice the normal butterfat content. It was an immediate sensation, so he quickly added other flavors. He had invented a super premium ice cream.

When summer came, he opened a beachfront ice cream stand, and that first summer he sold $60,000 worth of ice cream cones—at a nickel a cone. By 1928 he was selling $240,000 worth of ice cream cones. He kept adding flavors until he reached 28 varieties.

"I thought I had every flavor in the world," Howard remarked. "The 28 flavors became my trademark." He advertised it, truthfully, as "New England's Best Ice Cream," and his success reinforced what became the guiding principle of his business life: Quality sells.

Over the next few summers he added more beachfront stands, and decided to do for the lowly hot dog what he had done for the ice cream cone. Instead of using the normal hot dog stand method of slapping them on a greasy grill, and then wrapping them in stale buns, he invented the idea of clipping the frankfurters at both ends, notching them lengthwise, and then cooking them in pure creamery butter that would infuse into the meat. He used only the highest-quality meats (unheard of in those days) and lightly toasted, buttered fresh rolls. He had elevated the hot dog to connoisseur status, and it was to become one of the unforgettable joys of visiting Howard Johnson's restaurants for generations. Again, that little extra drive for quality would pay enormous dividends in the years to come.

His success was beginning to be noticed by others, and so he was able to convince some skeptical bankers to lend him enough money to open a restaurant in Quincy, Massachusetts. It was located in Quincy's first skyscraper—a 10-story granite art deco building that still looks magnificent today. This first Howard Johnson's restaurant featured fried clams, baked beans, chicken pies, those elegant frankfurters, and, of course, the now locally famous Howard Johnson's ice cream. He was restless to expand, but the stock market crashed, the Depression began, and the banks weren't lending money.

Then Howard had a remarkable idea, one that would change the course of American business enterprise. In 1935, he persuaded an acquaintance to open another "Howard Johnson's" restaurant in Orleans on Cape Cod under a franchise. Howard Johnson would design the space, create the menu, set the standards, and deliver the food and ice cream. The franchisee, under a license, would own the property and receive the bulk of the revenues. Howard, always a stickler for quality, demanded that the restaurant be run by his quality standards, or the contract was void and the franchisee would have to remove the Howard Johnson sign.

Seemingly overnight, out of the depths of the Depression, a phenomenal business success was born. By the following summer there were 17 Howard Johnson's restaurants. All were successful beyond anyone's wildest expectations. Paul Herbert, for instance, opened a 70-seat restaurant in Cambridge, putting up $10,000 as one-third the cost, the remainder to be financed over three years. Mr. Herbert hoped he would gross $60,000 a year, but he actually grossed $200,000 during the first 12 months. It was something of an understatement when he declared, "You're in a good business when you own a Howard Johnson franchise."

That sentiment was to be repeated by many hundreds of happy and wealthy franchisees. By the end of 1936 there were 39 more franchised restaurants.

Howard Johnson moved with lightning speed, for he had seen that the growing popularity of the automobile was sending millions of hungry Americans out on the road, and there were no decent places to satisfy their needs. He created the highway landmark concept, featuring the bright orange roof and the Simple Simon and the Pie Man road sign. By 1939 there were 107 Howard Johnson restaurants along East Coast highways generating revenues of $10.5 million.

All were run according to the "Howard Johnson Bible"—a set of strict standards of cleanliness, service, recipes, menu items, and quality (as well as interior and exterior design) that were developed and rigidly enforced by Howard Johnson himself. It was quite a voluminous bible, and it left nothing to chance. The author meticulously wrote every instruction on everything and anything that had to do with the running of his restaurants. He would allow no variation from one restaurant to the other. One chapter was devoted to the "Howard Johnson Waitresses—Your Appearance from Head to Toe." An entire page covered the subject of being courteous, including instructions on how to "assist customers with their wraps."

As the vast American highway system began to span the continent, millions of travelers, in their Ford "woody" station wagons and Chevy coupes, eagerly searched for the familiar orange roof and the big Howard Johnson sign with Simple Simon and the Pie Man on top.

They searched, and the kids clapped and cheered when they saw it, for they all knew exactly what they would find inside—the best fried clams anywhere, hot dogs grilled in butter and served on toasted rolls, old-fashioned chicken pot pie, generous turkey dinners with mashed potatoes, moist, rich brownies, games and puzzles for the kids, high chairs for the tots, and 28 flavors of the world's best ice cream. All served family style, by smiling waitresses in their prim, starched blue and orange dresses, all to be enjoyed in spanking clean, colorful surroundings.

Here was the nation's "Host of the Highway," where everyone invariably found a warm welcome, a familiar experience, and a special feeling that became part of growing up in America.

In less than 14 years, the dreamer who aspired to create a better ice cream cone now directed a mammoth franchise network of over 10,000 employees, with 170 restaurants, many serving a million and a half people a year.

And the heady beat went on.

The Pennsylvania, Ohio, and New Jersey turnpikes were built, and Howard Johnson bid and won exclusive rights to serve the hungry turnpike multitudes.

There were 200 Howard Johnson restaurants on the morning that America woke up to three huge black letters on the front page: WAR!

With World War II came gas rationing, food stamps, and the end of pleasure trips. One by one, the restaurants were forced to close. By the summer of 1944, only 12 remained in business. Howard managed to stay barely afloat by serving commissary food to war workers and army recruits. But by the time America was celebrating V-J Day, Howard Johnson was working late into the nights getting ready for the travel boom and the highway expansion that he knew had to be coming.

He was about to make one of the biggest comebacks in business history. After the war, America turned its incredible energy to building houses in a new world called "suburbia," building big, powerful cars that seemingly everyone could afford, and building the endless interstate highway system that connected the cities and the people, coast to coast. It was a world custom-made for our "pioneer of the highways" Howard Johnson. And he didn't waste a minute.

By 1947, construction was under way or about to begin on 200 new Howard Johnson restaurants that would stretch across the Southeast and Midwest. These were slightly smaller buildings than the prewar originals, but Howard Johnson still provided over 700 items, including his famous fried clams, saltwater taffy, and 28 flavors of ice cream. By 1951, Howard Johnson sales totaled $115 million.

By 1954, there were 400 Howard Johnson restaurants in 32 states. About 10 percent were company-owned turnpike restaurants that were extremely profitable. The orange roof just kept spreading until it rivaled Coca-Cola's trademark as the most familiar icon in America. And countless memories of family travel were born under every orange roof.

In 1959, the company founder, who still made his headquarters in Wollaston, Massachusetts, decided it was time to turn the reins over to his son, 26-year-old Howard Brennon Johnson, who succeeded him as president. Young Howard, a graduate of Andover and Yale, told a reporter, "I knew from the age of five that I wanted to join the company. It was all we talked about at home. And my father was the kind of person you almost couldn't let down." The senior Howard Johnson remained as chairman and treasurer, though he was now able to enjoy his 60-foot yacht and his growing art collection. He died in 1972, at the age of 76.

According to the International Franchise Association, most analysts estimate that franchising companies and their franchisees accounted for $1 trillion in annual U.S. retail sales from 320,000 franchised small businesses in 75 industries.

Today, franchising is a highly regulated industry offering a great opportunity to people who truly want to realize their dreams and go into business for themselves.

Franchising is evolving; it's getting better conceptually and in reality. There are greater opportunities for wealth creation among both franchisees and franchisors today then ever before.

The United States has experienced an explosion in franchising in the last two decades. The primary reason for this explosion is that franchising is the most efficient business model for distributing goods and services, and advanced free-market economies reward efficiency above all.

The growth of franchising is inevitable, because franchising clearly offers aspiring, new business owners the best possible chance of succeeding with the least risk. It is estimated that within a decade or less, franchising will comprise over 50 percent of the retail economy and will enable hundreds of thousands to realize the dream of successful business ownership.

As world economies and the move toward free-market economies grow, new franchise concepts will come on the scene and the solid, well-managed, existing franchise companies will continue to grow.

In the United States, franchising generates $1.53 trillion in economic output, and one of every seven jobs in the nation's private-sector economy. A study conducted by PricewaterhouseCoopers for the International Franchise Association on the economic impact of franchised businesses found there are more than 765,000 franchised small businesses in the United States, generating more than 18 million jobs.

> "When all is said and done, franchising is all about relationships."
>
> *Brad Sugars*

▌ What Is Franchising?

Did you know? _____

Pizza Hut opened its first company-owned restaurant in Wichita, Kansas, in 1958.

Pizza Hut opened its first franchise unit in Topeka, Kansas, in 1959.

Pizza Hut opened its first restaurant in Australia in 1970.

Mention the word franchising to anyone and chances are they'll immediately think of names such as Subway, KFC, and McDonald's. Funny how the "big guys," the internationals, always seem to spring to mind first. Then, after some reflection, names like Harvey Norman, Kwik Kopy, and VIP Home Services will roll off their lips. These are the larger, home-grown, true blue, Aussie success stories that everyone is familiar with. And then, of course, there is the local lawn mowing service that is truly a part of the local suburban scene.

But franchising goes far deeper than that. It is alive and well and operating in almost every business category in the economy, from banking to petroleum supplies, and from legal services to dog washing. One could almost be forgiven for thinking that franchising is the very cornerstone of the economy!

So what is franchising? Does a succinct definition exist?

A franchise can be defined as:

- Authorization given to somebody to sell or distribute a company's goods or services in a particular area.

- A business or group of businesses set up or operated specifically in accordance with an authorization.

- The territory or the limits within which the right to operate a business exists.

- A professional sports team.

Well, modern-day sporting teams are big business, aren't they?

The word franchise is actually a very old one, originating back in the fourteenth century, believe it or not. It meant free, or to make free. Isn't that interesting? If you think about it, the meaning has changed over time. It could be argued that today, it has acquired almost the opposite meaning!

Franchising is not a business itself, but a way of doing business. It is essentially a marketing concept—an innovative method of distributing goods and services. It is also an extremely successful and rapidly growing aspect of the small business sector of many countries.

But like everything in life, it's not as simple as it first appears. Franchising can be used to describe a number of business models, the most common being *business format franchising*. But there are other models that are also dependent on franchise relationships. These include:

1. Manufacturer-Retailer: where the retailer as a franchisee sells the franchisor's product directly to the public, such as new motor vehicle dealership.

2. Manufacturer-Wholesaler: where the franchisee, under license, manufactures and distributes the franchisor's product, such as in soft drink bottling arrangements.

3. Wholesaler-Retailer: where the retailer as a franchisee purchases products for retail sale from a franchisor wholesaler, such as in hardware and automotive product stores.

4. Retailer-Retailer: where the franchisor markets a service or a product under a common name and standardized system through a network of franchisees. This is the classic business format franchise.

In essence, franchising is a relationship between the franchisor: (the company selling the franchise) and the franchisee: (the person buying the franchise). Franchisees usually pay a franchise fee as well as royalties for their franchise, but more about this later.

Because franchising is a unique way of doing business, and it covers a very diverse range of businesses—some big and some small—the only way of ensuring the system doesn't self-destruct is to create a peak industry body to oversee virtually every facet of its operation. In Australia, this body is the Franchise Council of Australia, which represents franchisees, franchisors, and service providers to the sector. Its objectives are:

- To establish standards of international best practices in business format franchising for Australian franchise systems.

- To provide information and education about franchising to existing and potential franchisees and franchisors.

- To lobby state and federal governments on issues relevant to the sector.

- To develop a vital, strong, and financially viable franchising sector.

- To advance the interests of members in Australia and in special interest markets such as the International Franchise Community, Franchise Advisory Councils, Small Business Forums, and property leasing organizations (particularly shopping centers).

- To continually foster among consumers, governments, and the business community, a broad-based understanding of the economic importance of having a strong franchising sector in Australia

- To design efficient, identified, value-added services to members and assist them to be more effective in franchising.

As the peak body for franchising in Australia, the Franchise Council of Australia continues to add value to the businesses of its members by providing a range of services relevant to franchising and which represent good value. It is closely affiliated with franchising associations around the world, and is a founding member of the Asia Pacific Franchise Confederation. It is also a member of the World Franchise Council.

A Code of Conduct regulates the affairs of the industry, which is a mandatory industry code that regulates the conduct of participants in franchising towards other participants in franchising. In relation to franchise agreements concerning the retail marketing of motor fuel, it operates concurrently with the Petroleum

Retail Marketing Franchise Act 1980. The Code covers everything from disclosure to conditions for franchise agreement and dispute resolution. The Australian Federal Government amended the Franchising Code of Conduct by introducing the Trade Practices (Industry Code Franchising Amendment) Regulations 2001. The Regulations were made by the Governor General on the 28th of June 2001 and commenced on the 1st of October 2001.

So now you have a general idea of what franchising is all about. And you should also realize that it is a complex field that has many variations and permutations—no two franchise systems are exactly the same.

Let's now take a closer look at the scope and scale of franchising and what it means to the economy. I'm talking big picture here. This should put franchising in perspective.

"Franchising brings a great business idea together with people who have both the capital and the passion to run the business."

Brad Sugars

▊ How Big Is the Industry?

Did you know? ... _____

Australia is the most franchised nation per head of population in the world. That is, there are more franchise systems in Australia compared to its population than any other country, and Australia has at least three times as many franchise systems per head of population than the United States. *(Franchising Australia 2002, the Commonwealth Bank Franchising Survey)*

Franchising is an industry that is alive, well, and growing at a phenomenal rate. Its tentacles have spread into just about every corner of the economy.

Franchised businesses continue to grow in all corners of the world. Franchisors in many countries are increasingly establishing franchises across borders. More than 400 U.S. franchise systems operate internationally. International franchising has been successful because consumers around the world recognize famous brands as symbols of quality, consistency, service, and value.

As the economy becomes more service and technology oriented, as more women enter the work force, and as a larger percentage of the population grows older, growth areas in franchising are responding to these changes.

So let's take a closer look at the industry in the United States.

Chances are you may not realize how much franchises have become an integral part of your life. You could easily get goods and services from franchises on a daily basis without knowing it because the abundance of concepts and models is so great.

There are an estimated 1500 franchise companies operating in the United States doing business through more than 765,000 retail units. More than 70 different industries use franchising to distribute goods and services to consumers.

Of course, it would be just about impossible to give indicative figures here, but what I can say is that franchising is big business. The best information I have indicates that franchising now accounts for almost half of all U.S. retail sales, having a $1.5 trillion impact on the U.S. economy. It's bigger than the gross domestic product of China.

Take a moment to think about this—it's quite staggering. Think about the influence franchising has on our economy. Think about how many families rely on it for their livelihoods.

As major American franchise companies grow more competitive in the United States, many larger chains have looked to overseas markets for their future growth.

McDonald's is the leading restaurant brand, with more than 30,000 local restaurants serving nearly 50 million customers in more than 119 countries each day. Franchising is one of the more dependable generators of economic activity and will create new jobs every time a franchise expands or adds a new location.

OK, so how big is the franchise scene and how many people earn a living in the industry?

It is quite staggering, really. According to a study released by the IFA in March 2004, which measured the direct and indirect impact of franchise businesses, the total economic impact of franchising (which includes what occurs both in and because of franchises) resulted in more than 18.1 million jobs in the United States. But here is another important indicator: failure rates within the industry. According to the U.S. Small Business Administration, less than 5 percent of all franchise units fail each year. This is compared to 30 to 35 percent of small businesses that fail within the first year of operation.

OK, so what's the situation in other areas of the world?

Franchising has changed the landscape of world economies, affecting us in many ways. It is now a permanent part of the way we live, growing stronger with each passing year.

It would be fair to estimate that the franchise business model exists in 119 countries around the world. McDonalds leads the way in opening markets to the concept of franchising, and once established, others quickly follow.

There is no combined research on worldwide franchising, so I have provided a quick summary of franchising in a handful of countries across the globe:

Australia

Franchising in Australia is rapidly expanding. Latest statistics from the Franchise Council of Australia show that there are 850 franchise systems consisting of 50,600 franchised units nationally. Over 500,000 people are currently employed in a franchise system.

The growth has been massive considering there were only 184 franchise opportunities available in 1988. It is estimated that the franchise sector in Australia now accounts for nearly 4 percent of existing business numbers, however, it accounts for 30 percent of retail sales volume. Franchise sales have grown from $14 billion in 1987 to over $40 billion per annum in 1994 (Australian Bureau of Statistics). The growth is still continuing.

Canada

Canadians have embraced franchising wholeheartedly. There are approximately 1800 franchise systems operating in Canada with over 75,000 franchise outlets. Growth in the franchise industry has increased by 20 percent in the past 10 years.

Franchising in Canada employs over 1 million people, and approximately 50 percent of all retail expenditure takes place in a franchise outlet. Retail sales by franchised businesses are approximately $90 billion (BFA-Natwest Franchise Survey).

United Kingdom

Franchising growth in the United Kingdom also remains steady, the NatWest/British Franchising Association Survey reporting a 3 percent increase in franchise systems since 2003. There are now 718 franchise systems in operation with an estimated 327,000 people employed.

China

Statistics from the China Chain Stores and Franchise Association shows the franchise business model is prospering in China with more than 2000 franchise stores and over 120,000 outlets. Franchising employs approximately 1.8 million people, with more than 600,000 job opportunities created in 12 months. Sales turnover has grown by 41.5 percent since 2004.

South Africa

Franchising is emerging strongly in South Africa. The Franchise Association of Southern Africa reports 33 percent growth in franchising in 12 months. There are approximately 300 franchises and almost 10,000 outlets. Almost 30 percent of franchises in South Africa are represented by the fast food sector.

New Zealand

The Franchise Association of New Zealand estimates there are over 300 franchise systems in New Zealand with 14,000 outlets. There are roughly 70,000 people employed in franchising, with an annual turnover of $10 billion. The fastest-growing sectors are in Business and Property Services, Construction and Trade, and Personal and Other Services.

Japan

Franchising in Japan has seen steady growth in recent years. There are currently 1061 franchise systems consisting of approximately 227,000 franchise outlets. Franchising in Japan employs more than 2 million people.

Hungary

The Hungarian Franchise Association estimates there are 400 franchise systems operating in Hungary, approximately 50 percent of which are foreign owned. The share of franchises in the retail sector is estimated to increase by 10–12 percent over the next five years.

> "Most businesses that fail in franchising do so because they don't have the margin for the franchisees to make a profit after the franchise fee."
>
> *Brad Sugars*

▌The Nature of Franchising

Did you know? _____

The Athlete's Foot was established in 1971 in Pittsburgh, Pennsylvania. It is the world's first, and largest, franchisor of athletic footwear.

The Athlete's Foot is a privately owned subsidary of Groupe Rallye, a French food retail conglomerate that has interests in fashion, home improvements, sport, and real estate.

The Athlete's Foot has 600 stores in 48 countries, including 107 in Australia and New Zealand. The first international franchise store opened in 1978 in Adelaide, Australia, the beginning of The Athelete's Foot International expansion.

_____

Not all franchise systems are the same. Seems like an obvious observation, but there's more to it than meets the eye. Just because a company has chosen the franchise route doesn't mean its basic way of operating or conducting business will be the same as other franchises.

This is one of the common misconceptions about franchising. To be successful in the world of franchising, this is the very first thing you need to understand.

Think of it like baking a cake. There are many different recipes you could use to bake a cake. They all have the same objective in mind—a cake. But they probably take different routes. You see, one may call for the ingredients to be mixed and then placed in the microwave oven. Another might use the same ingredients, only this time they are to be placed in a cake tin in the oven. Yet others may use premixed ingredients, and all you need to do is to add water. But they all produce the same cake. Now we could go further and say that some recipes are for chocolate cakes while others are for cream sponge cakes. But I think you get the idea.

Franchising is the same. There are various routes a franchised business can take to profitability. There are different business recipes it can follow. These are called models.

The interesting thing to note about these different models is that they hinge around the differing relationships that exist between the franshisor and the franchisee. And remember, in franchising, these relationships are fundamental to the ultimate success or failure of the business experience.

OK, so what are these models?

Modern franchising revolves around two main models: Product/Trade Name Franchises and the Business Format Franchise. There are others, and those will be discussed briefly a little later on. First, let's have a closer look at the two major types.

Product/Trade Name Franchises

When you come to think of it, the very reason for existing for many businesses is to sell a product or a range of products. It's the product that occupies center stage here.

Let's take the motor industry as an example. The Ford Motor Company manufactures a range of motor vehicles to satisfy particular motoring needs in the market. How does it get these vehicles to its customers? Does it sell them directly to the motoring public? No, it supplies stock to motor dealerships, which do the selling. They are the middlemen that become the "face" of the company as far as the buying public is concerned. It is the dealership that the customer has contact with.

These dealerships "look" as though they are part of the Ford Motor Company, but they aren't. You see, although they display all the outward appearances of the Ford Motor Company, they are in actual fact privately owned franchises of the Ford Motor Company.

It's primarily the product and the trade name that are paramount here. These are the visible manifestations of the business arrangement.

So what are the important features of a product/trademark franchise? It all comes down to the type, or nature, of the business relationship that exists between the franchisor on the one hand and the franchisee on the other.

In these instances, the franchisor remains very much more relaxed about the way in which the franchisee goes about selling its product. This does not mean there are little or no operational standards that must be met—there are—but the franchisee is very much more in control of these functions than in other models.

The franchisor usually derives profit from the ongoing supply of the product to its franchisees and from the up-front fee payable to secure the rights to sell the product and use the trade name in the first place. Advice and ongoing support in the areas of product knowledge, training, service, advertising, and promotion are usually also supplied to franchisees.

Now if you had a Product/Trade Name franchise, it wouldn't necessarily mean that you were a middleman or a distributor. You could be a manufacturer too, manufacturing a franchisor's product under licence. This is a very popular arrangement, especially in the food and beverage sector. The product would still be the major focal point and the franchisee would still enjoy a very high level of independence. Soft drink bottling companies are a good example.

Business Format Franchise

The other major franchise model is known as the Business Format Franchise. This is the model that most people would be thinking of when the word franchise is mentioned. This is, of course, purely coincidental, because most people wouldn't really know what distinguishes the one model from the other. Let's hope that in a few minutes, you won't be able to count yourself as one of them!

So what are the main distinguishing characteristics of this model, then? For starters, the relationship between the franchisor and the franchisee is very much more rigid. It is very much more prescribed. You see, when people buy these franchises, they are buying a complete and comprehensive system. The franchisor has developed not only a great product, but also an entire and comprehensive system through which to take it to market. The franchisee is, therefore, buying not only the right to sell the product and make use of the trade name or trademark, but also goodwill, product and marketing knowledge, intellectual property, marketing and promotion power, ongoing training, quality control, operational policies and procedures, research and development, assistance, guidance, support, and bulk buying muscle. This is very much a turnkey operation—just put the key in the door, turn it, walk in, and begin operating.

The franchisor usually derives profit from the initial up-front fee paid by the franchisee for access to the franchisor's intellectual property, and then an ongoing fee, which can be based on turnover or some other determining factor. The franchisee also contributes to an advertising and marketing fund—as a percentage of monthly turnover.

The working relationship is strictly laid out in the franchise agreement. The franchisee must conduct business strictly in accordance with the system, as detailed in the policy and procedures manual. While many franchisees may regard this as the down side of this model of franchising, the quid pro quo is that the franchisee receives a much greater level of support than working under the Product/Trade Name franchise model.

The advantage of this model, particularly from the franchisor's point of view, is that standardization, uniformity, and consistency are key principles in the business philosophy. The franchisor maintains control of certain key business functions, while the franchisee is able to "behave" like a big company, but with the budget of a small company. They get more bang for their bucks.

Other Models

Due to the very nature of the business world, things are never cut and dried. Things are seldom straightforward and simple. Differing situations and business considerations have resulted in unique solutions being developed to suit particular requirements.

The world of franchising is no different. Consequently you may come across franchise arrangements that, in reality, are more like independent distribution agreements, commissioned agencies, joint ventures, or a combination of some of these. And some franchisors operate a mixture consisting of company-owned branches or dealerships, joint ventures, and franchises. Who said business was boring?

"Remember that if you franchise a bakery, you're no longer in the bakery business; you're in the franchising business."

Brad Sugars

PART 2

▋ So You Want to Buy a Franchise, Do You?

Did you know? _____

Colonel Sanders actively began franchising his chicken business in 1952 at the age of 65.

When he sold his interest in the U.S. company for $2 million in 1964, he had more than 600 franchised outlets in the United States and Canada.

Today, there are more than 11,000 KFC stores in more than 80 countries. They serve eight million customers each day.

Next to owning your own home, owning your own business has got to be the one thing most people aspire to. Both are underpinned by that sense of freedom, of not being controlled by others, that is at the heart of our very own identity.

Being in control of your time, your effort, and, hopefully, your income are very powerful driving forces. There is something about being self-employed that appeals to the vast majority of us, even though to most, it will sadly remain a dream.

Let's explore the notion of being *self-employed*. What does it actually mean and what, if any, are the characteristics of the self-employed?

This is usually the first jump on the entrepreneurial ladder and for most, it's the only jump. In fact, most entrepreneurs never seem to get past this level of growth in their business.

The truth is you really can't call it a business; you've really got to call it a *job*.

What's more, this job is most probably one of the worst jobs in the world. I think it's put best by this quote, taken from one of my live seminars: "Most people thought they worked for an idiot *before* they started their own business."

I really don't think most people who start their own businesses know what they're getting themselves into. In fact, most look at it as something glamorous, exciting, and with such a sense of newfound freedom they're fooled into believing wealth is just a few days, weeks, or months away.

To become self-employed, what usually happens is one of two things:

Either you're unemployed and looking for a new job when one morning you have what I call a Blinding Flash of the Obvious.

"I know," you say, "I'll start my own business. Then no one will ever be able to fire me."

And with all of the planning of the team that built and sailed the Titanic, you get started.

Or you're working for someone else and you keep thinking these three things to yourself:

"I can do a better job myself."

"How come they get *all* the money, when I do all the work?" and,

"If I owned this company, I'd be the boss; I'd make everyone else do the work; I'd play golf, relax, and I'd work a lot less."

Either way, there is one thing running through the minds of everyone as they jump into the role of the self-employed entrepreneur:

"I'm going to be the boss."

And with that the race starts.

It's one of the biggest steps you'll ever take, and believe me, the most rewarding you'll ever choose, so if you're about to take it, that's great. Get ready to learn how to make it work for you.

Almost an extension of the mind-set challenges we've just looked at, most self-employed people's relationships with money need to be examined.

As you may or may not know, the way you relate to money will determine your financial future. And, given you've only got one shot at this thing called life, let's make sure you give it the best shot you can.

A self-employed person has a very similar relationship to money as that of an employee. And we all know that as an employee you *earn* money. What kind of word is *earn*? It's a verb or *do*ing word.

With the self-employed, the word changes but the *do*ing-ness remains the same. They're still trading time for money. And their word in relation to bringing in money is now, *make*.

They have to *make* money in their business.

The dictionary definition of "make" is: "To bring into existence, especially by effort."

So by definition, with this relationship to money you're still going to be working hard for every dollar you get. You're still trading time for money. Yes, you may be getting more dollars for each hour you work, but the see-saw effect of self-employment never lets you create financial freedom. More on that in a moment.

While we're on definitions, here's the definition for "self:" "Person's nature, special qualities, one's own personality."

And the definition for "employed:" "Give work to, usually for payment."

Once again by definition you've positioned yourself in a place that from a true entrepreneur's viewpoint is not only guaranteed to mean physical involvement in your money-making activities, but also that there's very little difference to being employed by someone else.

The only real difference is now you have the headaches of being both an employee and an employer.

Yet, I want you to remember this: becoming self-employed is the first step on the ladder of financial freedom, and those who have taken it are usually far closer to becoming financially free than those who never do.

So, congratulations if you have, and congratulations in advance if you're about to.

Now it's time to think through some of the reasons people have for becoming self-employed. And they must be powerful ones, considering all the uncertainty and hard work most will be putting themselves through.

So what are they?

To my mind there are at least eight very powerful reasons for being self-employed. Reasons that, simply put, are a must if you're at all serious about getting yourself into the ranks of the *rich.*

Employees have absolutely no true leverage; they're simply trading time for dollars. Keep this in mind.

When you're selling for yourself, there's no set hourly rate. You, through your skills, your level of work, and your passion or determination, are able to determine your level of income. No one else can make that decision for a self-employed person. And, while that scares some, it feels great to many who take this step.

In fact, that level of self-control promised by the "I did it my way" feeling is central to the decision most people make when becoming self-employed. While being your own boss, and the ability to determine your own hours and income, are seen as the main reasons why anyone would choose to become self-employed, they are not the reasons I would give you to make this step.

So, what are my reasons for becoming self-employed?

Reason 1 You'll have to learn about company structure and setup. You'll probably also need to understand the difference between a holding company and a trading company. Why you should always have two companies rather than one: one to own the assets, the other to trade and make the ongoing profits.

Reason 2 You'll also need to learn accounting, bookkeeping, and how to interact with your accountant. You may, for the first time in your life, get yourself an accountant.

Knowing where to look for the answers to your questions about the balance sheet, the profit and loss statement, the cashflow, or any budgets you do is a must if you're ever to aspire to bigger and better things.

Think of accounting as a background part of day-to-day business; it's like the engine room. Without it you may as well be playing sport and not keeping score.

Reason 3 Probably the most important two things you'll ever learn as a self-employed person (if you didn't already as an employee) is sales and marketing.

Becoming a great salesperson is a must if you're going to sell a lot. Sales means everything from face-to-face, over the phone, cold calling, and even getting over any fear you may have of talking to people. Sales also means doing presentations to groups and selling to more than one person at a time.

It's easy to say, but becoming great at sales requires a lot of reading, learning, and application. It may even take you a few years, if you've never done it before as an employee.

And marketing, well what can I say that hasn't already been said? Together with sales, it's the lifeblood of any business. A true entrepreneur knows that, while cost reduction is important, bringing in the cashflow is by far the most important area for any company.

You can cut costs to post a profit, but you can only sell your way to prosperity. While "sales" is the ability to turn a lead into a sale, "marketing" is the ability to generate prospects at a reasonable price. Read my books from the Instant Success series—*Instant Cashflow, Instant Leads, Instant Promotions, Instant Sales, Instant Repeat Business,* and *Instant Advertising*—to make sure you know the best marketing information there is.

Reason 4 As a new business owner, you get the privilege of doing everything yourself, and one thing you really get to learn is the meaning of the words "hard work." You'll often complete 16- or 20-hour days, six or seven days a week. Not because there is just so much work to do, but because you're having fun, you're learning, growing and most of all, because you're working out how to design a business as you go along. Growing a business is like riding a bike: Once you've done it a few times, it gets really easy.

Think of all this extra work as your entrepreneurial apprenticeship being done after hours.

Reason 5 One of the most important lessons every new business owner learns is cost reductions. As a self-employed person, you'll be forced to scrimp and save, to recycle, to borrow, to use old secondhand stuff and to do whatever it takes to get by.

Once again, while it's most important for a company to bring in money, lack of control over your costs is a certain death knock for a small business. Learning this "tight" way of doing business is great; you'll need to remember it, especially as you get bigger.

Reason 6 for becoming self-employed is to simply make contacts. The more people network, the easier you'll find it to do business—any business. Or, to put it another way, join as many networking groups as you can, go to as many seminars as you can, to not only learn, but to get yourself out there meeting other businesspeople.

In business, the old axiom of "who you know" is extremely important, so learn to meet lots of people.

Reason 7 As a self-employed person, you'll also have to relearn the meaning of responsibility and accountability. Nowhere else is it as important to learn these virtues than as the boss of your own company. The "buck" really does start and stop with you.

Far too often the world of the employee is littered with "pass the buck" people. When these people start or buy their own businesses, it's almost certain that they'll fail. Only those with the passion and desire to lead a life of total ownership will ever succeed in their own businesses.

Reason 8 Of course, another great reason for becoming self-employed is to make more money. Usually good employees will make a whole lot more money as self-employed business owners. This is not just because they're making more, but because of all the appropriate and legal tax deductions they can claim, the fact that they pay tax only on their profits and not on their entire wage, and the fact that they get to pay tax later than an employee would.

To top it all off, people seem to work harder when they know the dollars are going into their own pockets and not someone else's.

Reason 9 The most important reason is so you at least start to learn technology. Hopefully, like many others, you learned these lessons at someone else's expense as an employee, but if not, prepare for a lot of learning and growth as you get your first company up and running at a profit.

Technology is here to stay and it's a painful business life for people who decide not to make it an integral part of their knowledge base.

To finish off—while most think the reasons for becoming self-employed are to take control and to be the boss, the exact opposite is true for the serious entrepreneur.

Start your small business now, even if it's part-time, to gain the knowledge you'll need in a few years when you're playing with big dollars and running your big business.

Now, before I forget—

Remember I mentioned a concept called the see-saw of the self-employed?

As a self-employed person, your business life will feel just like a see-saw. While it's often true self-employed people can make more per hour than they ever could as an employee, the challenge comes down to how many hours are actually used in the background.

You'll spend half your life chasing the work doing marketing, sales, and administration, and then you'll have so much work to do you'll have to flip over and start doing the work.

Doing the work is one side of the see-saw and sales and marketing is the other.

Chase the work, do the work, chase the work, do the work, chase the work, do the work—and so on.

It's this see-saw that stops a self-employed person from ever really getting ahead. Once again, you're still in a situation where there's no real leverage. You still need to *do* the work.

It's also this see-saw that gets most self-employed people to make one of two decisions: to either give it up and go back and get jobs, or to take the plunge, jump in the deep ends of businesses, make the decision to grow their businesses, and to hire team members.

You see, what you should be aiming at here is to grow your business.

The first step to doing this is to think about your vision. Understand that as long as you can only ever see yourself running a one-person business, you'll never be anything more.

You've got to build a vision of a big business, one that needs to be big to achieve the vision you set. Maybe your vision is to change the world, to change your industry, or to be the best in your industry. Whatever your vision, the bigger it is, the bigger your business needs to become to complete it.

Set a vision of what your business will be like when you've finished building it. You see, you have to plan it from the start so at some stage in the near future, your business will run without you. Plan for it from the beginning.

While we're on change, one of the most important changes you'll need to make is to your identity. You'll have to stop thinking of yourself as a worker and start thinking of yourself as a business owner.

For example, you may need to stop thinking of yourself as a plumber and become the owner of a plumbing business—an entrepreneur who's currently building a plumbing business. Or, you may have to remember to stop telling people you're a hairdresser and start thinking of yourself as the owner of a growing hairdressing empire.

One other thing here; stop thinking of yourself or your business as being *small*. Calling yourself a small business is extremely limiting. You can be a growth business, a prototype business, or even think of yourself as a big business. Don't just change your own identity; change the identity of your business as well.

I know this all seems overly simplistic, and it could even be just a mind game, but it's by far the most important step you need to take on your way to becoming a successful business owner. Set your vision as soon as you can.

The next step you need to take is to change your goals.

Set larger goals, much larger goals. Ask for more and then be prepared to get it. There's nothing worse than the limits you place upon yourself by setting small goals. Goals that may at the time seem a stretch in reality might just get you to work a little harder.

You see, when you set goals that are entirely massive compared with your current results, it challenges you to think entirely differently and to do things entirely differently. And that in itself is essentially what this growth process is all about.

So there you have it—a quick overview of what being self-employed is all about. Still convinced this is the route for you to take?

Congratulations, you've just taken one of the biggest and most important decisions you'll ever make. Now all you still need to do is to decide *how* you'll get into business for yourself.

In the Introduction to this book, I outlined the three ways you can go about it. I also mentioned that there are compelling reasons for choosing the franchise option, in preference to a stand-alone business. The most important of these is that many of the pitfalls of starting up in business have been removed. Someone else has already tested and measured all the variables for you. Everything has been set up ready to go. And although you'll feel like you're out there "doing your own thing," you'll not be left to your own devices. You'll have a well-constructed safety net there to catch you if you fall. You'll be able to concentrate your efforts on doing what it takes to generate cashflow without having your mind and energy diverted to deal with "housekeeping" or behind-the-scenes issues that do not directly influence the amount of business you attract.

Buying a franchise is a terrific way to get into business without the risks involved in starting one up for yourself. It is well known that the failure rate of businesses, especially during the establishment phase, is very high indeed. According to the U.S. Small Business Administration, about one-third of new businesses fail in the first two years of operations, with about half surviving at least four years. The average failure rate of franchised businesses is less than 5 out of every 100.

A 1997 Gallup Organization study of franchise owners on their attitudes towards their franchise experience revealed that two of three respondents said they would not have been successful if they had tried to open the same business on their own.

Isn't that interesting?

Being a franchisee could be thought of as something like a cross between being self-employed and being an employee. You have the best of both worlds. You get to enjoy freedom, to be your own boss, and to run your own show, yet with the security offered by being an employee. That's the beauty of it.

But it has to be pointed out that franchising is certainly not a bed of roses. Like anything else in life, it has advantages as well as disadvantages and it is up to you to weigh the pros and cons for yourself. We all have different views about what level of risk we should take in business—some people are comfortable with higher levels of risk-taking than others. It all depends on your own particular situation.

So what do you have to weigh up when deciding whether the franchise option is the route to take? What kind of factors should you evaluate according to your own business plans and ambitions?

Let's think about some of the *advantages* first.

The first advantage of buying a franchise is the training you receive. You don't have to be a specialist in the field before you go into business for yourself, as you would if you were to open up a business by yourself in that same field.

Then there's the security offered by the franchisor. You're not alone. You will be able to tap into a wealth of knowledge and experience to help you overcome any challenges you're going to be confronted with along the way. And the level of risk you'll be operating with will be significantly reduced.

You'll be able to start out in business under the umbrella of an already well-established brand name, image, and reputation. This won't apply, of course, if the franchise system itself is brand new. In this case, you should expect to buy in at considerably lower prices because you will be taking a larger business risk.

You won't need as much working capital by buying a franchise because the system will already have been streamlined and you'll be benefiting from the system's bulk buying power.

Another valuable advantage lies in the systems you'll be buying. You won't have to spend time and money developing them for yourself. And if business premises are involved, all the legalities, council requirements, red tape, and other bureaucratic requirements are taken care of.

National advertising and promotional campaigns are very expensive, but with a franchise, you'll get it all for a very small fee. This level of promotion is very powerful indeed, and extremely hard to quantify.

You also get the benefits associated with the franchisor's patents, trademarks, copyrights, trade secrets, and their ongoing research and development campaigns (if applicable). Any new developments will be passed on to you at the earliest opportunity. This very often gives franchisees a real market advantage.

Ongoing market research is also usually shared with franchisees. You see, it's just as much in the franchisor's interest as it is in yours that you have a marketing edge.

Another advantage could be that you get to operate in an exclusive territory or sales area. Now this isn't always the case, but where it is, it can give you a greater share of the existing market.

And one final advantage that's well worth considering: finance. You see, banks have long recognized the advantages of franchise companies and have tailored financial packages for franchisees that are far more attractive than those commonly available to other business owners.

These positives need to be considered against the following general negatives:

Most franchisees will be operating under a set of rigid controls or operating requirements that form part of the Franchise Agreement. You will not be free to do exactly what you please. Performance levels, standards, and other constraints will apply. To thrive (and in actual fact, to even survive) you will need to develop good communication and relationship skills. You will need to get along well with your franchisor.

You need to factor into your budgets the fact that you will be required to pay ongoing fees to your franchisor. These fees may be based on sales, turnover, or they could be set at a particular amount.

Many prospective franchisees will also be at a disadvantage when it comes to trying to assess the quality of the franchisor. How can you really go about this? Should you take their word for it or should you conduct your own searches? How do you verify their figures? How relevant are the stories they will tell you? You could ask existing franchisees, but how will you know who the most representative ones are? Every franchise system has its high-flyers, its mediocre performers, and its battlers. And if the truth be known, every system also has a core of disgruntled franchisees—those that blame everything, but themselves, for their situation. The last thing you'd want is to make contact with one of these while carrying out your due diligence. Yet you probably wouldn't want to talk to a high-flyer either, as you'd probably walk away with unrealistic expectations. This is a very real problem to which there is no easy answer. You'll just have to do the best you can and trust your instincts.

Another negative factor concerns how you go about selling your franchise. You see, most franchise agreements will have strict conditions relating to whom you can sell your business to. The prospective purchaser still needs to be acceptable to the franchisor and will have to pass the same tests or requirements as you did. So while this may not influence how you run your business, it nevertheless is a restriction that limits your freedom. You do not have the final say.

This "loss in independence" can have another potentially harmful consequence, and it can, in the franchise system, lead to the franchisee becoming too reliant on the franchisor, even for day-to-day operational matters. The franchisees can, over time, become lulled into a sense of false security which will, if left unchecked, rob them of their entrepreneurial spirit that lead to the decision to buy the franchise in the first place. They could lose their spark or zest for business, which will end up being detrimental to the business in no time at all.

And finally, a huge disadvantage lies in the fact that if the franchisor should go belly up, so will you. You might be running your franchise according to plan, but if the majority of others don't, you could pay the ultimate price. And there's no denying the fact that there have been unscrupulous franchisors in the past, and there will probably continue to be in the future.

These are some of the factors you need to weigh up before taking the plunge and signing on the bottom line.

> "To succeed in franchising, it is imperative that you can work with the people within your system."
>
> *Brad Sugars*

PART 3

▌ The Business Mind-Set

Did you know? _____

McDonald's Corporation is the world's largest chain of fast-food restaurants. The company began in 1940 with a restaurant opened by brothers Dick and Mac McDonald, but it was their introduction of the "Speedy Service System" in 1948 that established the principles of the fast-food restaurant.

In 1961 the McDonald brothers agreed to sell Ray Kroc business rights to their operation of $2.7 million. The agreement allowed the brothers to keep their original restaurant, but an oversight caused them to lose rights to the name. Had the brothers maintained their original agreement, they and their heirs would have been collecting in excess of $100 million per year today.

The McDonald's Corporation's business model is slightly different from that of most other fast-food chains. In addition to ordinary franchise fees, supplies, and percentage of sales, McDonald's also collects rent, partially linked to sales. As a condition of the franchise agreement, McDonald's owns the property on which most McDonald's franchises are located. McDonald's now owns more land in the world than any other corporation.

McDonald's trains its franchisees at Hamburger University in Oak Brook, Illinois. More people are trained by McDonald's every year than by the U.S., British, and Australian militaries combined. According to *Fast Food Nation* by Eric Schlosser (2001), nearly one in eight workers in the United States has at some time been employed by McDonald's.

Before you jump in and buy yourself a franchise, there's one very important question you need to ask yourself: "Do I have the mind-set of an entrepreneur?"

You see, whether you make it or not in business all comes down to one fundamental characteristic that you absolutely must have, and that's the mind-set of a businessperson.

If you don't have that natural, inbuilt nose for business, you're going to struggle to run your own business. You need to constantly strive for profitability, which means you need to have a keen eye on the five main business areas that together influence whether your business will be profitable or not. These areas are what I call The Business Chassis.

Most people don't really understand business and, therefore, they work too hard. In fact, most businesspeople work on the three areas of the chassis that refer to results, instead of the areas that can transform the business into a profit powerhouse. You'll see what I mean in a minute. First, let me explain the parts of the chassis. Think of it as the formula for success.

Your Number of Leads

This is the total number of potential buyers that you contacted or that contacted you last year. It's also known as prospects, or potentials. Most businesspeople confuse responses, or the number of potential buyers, with results. Just because the phone is ringing doesn't mean the cash register is. What's even more amazing is that very few businesses even know how many leads they get a week, let alone from each and every marketing campaign. It's great to get a lot of leads, but then you've got to remember your conversion rate.

Conversion Rate

This is the percentage of people who did buy as opposed to those who could have bought. For example, if you had 10 people walk through your store today and you sold to only 3 of them, you'd have a conversion rate of 3 out of 10, or 30 percent. This has to be a literal goldmine in almost every business I walk into. You've already got them interested; now you've just got to get them over the line. When I ask the business owners about their conversion rates, they take a stab in the dark and tell me that it's between 60 and 70 percent. Just for fun, I get them to measure it, and a couple of weeks later we find that it's more like 20 or 30 percent. Imagine how you would feel.

You should feel great; in fact you should be excited, because if you're getting by at 20 or 30 percent, imagine how your business would run at 60 or 70 percent. Remember, double your conversion rate and you've just doubled your turnover.

Your Number of Customers

This is the number of different customers you deal with. You work it out by multiplying the total number of leads by the conversion rate. Remember, *it's not about getting more customers*; you can't change that number. It's about getting more leads and then improving your conversion rate. These are the variables that lead to the result.

Your Number of Transactions

Some of your customers will buy from you weekly, others monthly, others on the odd occasion, and others just once in a lifetime. What you want to know now is the average. Not your best and not your worst, but the average number of times your customers buy from you in a year. Once again, here's another goldmine; most businesspeople never collect a database of their past customers, let alone write to them, or call them and ask them to come back.

Your Average Dollar Sale

Here's one variable that at least some business owners do measure. Once again, some might spend $5000, some just $5, but the average is what you're after. Just a few dollars on each and every sale could be all it takes to calculate. Add up your total dollar sales and divide it by the number of sales.

Your Turnover

This is another result. Multiply the total number of customers you dealt with, by the number of times they came back on average, and then by the average amount they spent with you each time. That's your turnover. Put simply, Customers x Transactions x Average $$$ Sale = Turnover. This is another area most business owners will know the answer to. Yet they most probably have no real idea how they got to it. Of course, you want more of it, but *you can't get more turnover*; what you can get is more transactions, and a higher average dollar sale with the total number of customers you deal with.

Your Margins

This is the percentage of each and every sale that's profit. In other words, if you sold something for $100 and $25 was profit, then you've got a 25 percent margin. Remember, this is after all costs have been taken out. It's potentially another little goldmine for you to tap into.

Your Profits

Another result that every business owner wants more of, not realizing that *you can't get more profit*. What you can get is get greater margins on the turnover you've got.

And that's it.

The Business Chassis is the basic model that dictates the profit levels of every business on earth.

By simply breaking down your business and marketing efforts *(selling is married to marketing)* into these five areas and understanding how each affects the other, you're halfway there—and way ahead of 90 percent of businesses out there.

Figure 3-1 shows what The Business Chassis looks like.

Does the thought of increasing your level of profitability send your pulse racing? Do you find the whole concept of increasing how much you make by tweaking the various variables in The Business Chassis fascinating? Has it already sent your mind into overdrive? Have you already identified a few things you just can't wait to try out? If the answer to these simple questions was in the affirmative, then you may have what it takes.

LEADS
(prospects or potential customers)

X

CONVERSION RATE
(the difference between those that could have bought and those that did)

=

CUSTOMERS
(the number of different customers you deal with)

X

NUMBER OF TRANSACTIONS
(the average number of times each customer bought from you that year)

X

AVERAGE DOLLAR SALE PRICE
(the average price of the items you sell)

=

TOTAL REVENUE
(the total turnover of the business)

X

MARGINS
(the percentage of each sale that's profit)

=

PROFIT
(something every business owner wants more of)

If, on the other hand, you are currently working for a boss, you still might have what it takes. But you do need to be aware that when you are your own boss, your entire approach to business will be very different to what it was when you were an employee. You see, you'll no longer instinctively reach for a new ream of paper when your photocopy machine runs empty. You'll think twice—or three times—before you raid your stationery cupboard. You'll most probably first check to see if you have any recycled paper you can use—paper that you have already printed on one side but decided not to use. You know the stuff; it's that paper you would previously have thrown into the bin. You will very soon begin to realize that, when you're running your own business, every cent you spend comes out of your own pocket. And this means potentially lower profits. You'll see things in a new light. You'll question everything.

Does this sound like you?

If you're still not sure, let's delve a little deeper into the mind-set of an entrepreneur.

But first, let's quickly discuss the word entrepreneur. What exactly is an entrepreneur? Entrepreneur can be defined as a person who organizes a business venture and assumes the risk for it. All entrepreneurs aren't the same. There are different types of entrepreneurs. That should be obvious to you, but why exactly are they different?

The way I describe it is like this; they operate on five different levels. Let me now explain the way their minds work at these levels. And I'll start off by explaining the mind-set of an employee first, because this will help highlight very clearly to you whether you have the mind-set of a businessperson or not.

The Entrepreneurial Mind-Set of the Level Zero—The Employee

There are so many fundamental thought patterns that show up in a group of employees. Some are extremely rare and others are a part of almost every employee you meet.

I'm just going to examine their five biggest beliefs that relate directly to money, wealth, and becoming an entrepreneur. Remember, every thought pattern or belief that you have in some way assists you and in others limits you. Something that may make you a great employee will truly limit you as an entrepreneur.

Friends invited me over for dinner recently. They had also invited some other friends of theirs. Several of them turned out to be serious employees.

They would ask questions like: "Who do you work for?" "How much do you earn?" But the one I liked most of all was: "What car do you drive?"

Now, I don't mean to be rude, but to some I will be. These people fell into the category I call "*looking good, going nowhere.*"

They would rather look rich than be rich. Another way to describe their lives would be to say that they live them secondhand. They do everything to build an impression of themselves to the outside world, and when the outside world says it's true, they believe it—even though it's just an illusion they've created. A secondhand opinion.

So, often just changing a couple of simple thoughts or beliefs could dramatically affect not only their financial lives, but also their emotional lives.

With this in mind, let's find the essential beliefs that have them and other level-zero employees trapped in that little mouse's wheel—always running, yet standing still.

First, the belief is that "*stuff*" is more important than *wealth*.

And, you know the "*stuff*" I'm alluding to. It's that dress you bought last week that you really didn't need. Those new Nike running shoes you bought because you liked the colors. The *stuff* you want, the *stuff* that chews up all your money, the *stuff* that seems *so* important when you're buying it…the *stuff* that rarely matters when you realize you're actually broke.

I'll be as blunt as I can. Spend your entire life buying *stuff* and you'll end up with *stuff all.*

Remember this; people should be first on your priority scale, money and wealth second, and *stuff*—or things—a very distant third.

Now, don't get me wrong. I own *lots* of *stuff,* but it's in proportion. I also have lots of investments, cash, businesses, properties, and so on. *Wealth* pays for my stuff whether I get out of bed or not.

By the way, whenever you want to buy *stuff*, you should learn how to make it a tax deduction.

Keep your "*stuff*" in perspective. Sure, have it, but don't become obsessed with it.

Onto the second level-zero belief we need to look at: Your income is representative of your wealth.

I think I've already beaten this one with a stick, but just in case I haven't made my case absolutely clear, let me go over it again.

Your income and your wealth are two entirely separate, and in most cases, nonrelated items. I've met people who make over a million dollars a year in salary, yet they are still poor because they spend more than that million on *stuff*.

I've met a 22-year-old young man who's never made more than $18,000 a year before tax and who has a net worth in excess of half a million dollars in his property portfolio.

Your income doesn't determine your wealth. It's what you do with your income that determines your wealth.

Remember, income does not equal wealth.

The third belief I want to examine and discard is this: Because I'm more intelligent, more skilled, or more experienced, I have a higher chance of becoming wealthy.

Once again, I've met a lot of very poor professors and very rich high-school dropouts.

For some reason we've come to equate good grades, good training, or good skills as the key ingredient to success. This is especially so in the world of the level-zero employee.

An entrepreneur knows that courage, taking action, and leadership are more important than scholastic intelligence.

In my world, my team of business coaches and I are continually working with people who "thought they knew everything about business." Remember this:

Nothing beats hard work, integrity, people skills, sales skills, and the desire to take a risk or two to turn it all into reality.

This clearly brings us to the fourth (and by far the most challenging) belief most employees struggle with: the security of the steady paycheck.

What's more secure—a business with one customer who buys everything you produce, or a business with tens of thousands of customers who each buy a small portion of what you produce, and who keep coming back to buy more?

Of course it's not the one with a single customer. The *job*, with just one boss, even though it feels like it's more secure, is not.

One of the biggest challenges I have when working with level-zero employees is that they make their decisions based on fear—on what could go wrong—rather than on vision, trust, and on what can go right.

Fear, in almost all cases, is the one thing stopping people from making the leap from level zero to level one and beyond.

This introduces the reason for fear, or belief number five on our hit list: "I don't know enough to start my own business."

Jumping from level zero into the world of business requires a fundamental shift in thinking. It requires a shift from a thought process of fear to a thought process of trust.

Trust in yourself.

By trusting you'll learn along the way; by trusting you'll make mistakes, but you will learn that you can recover. The only way to truly learn how to be an entrepreneur is to just get started.

Remember, fear of the unknown is natural. But living a life without the courage to step through your fears is unnatural.

All greatness follows a leap of faith, a courageous step into the unknown, into a world of new things, new challenges, and new possibilities.

Understand this; anyone can make the jump from level zero to level one. It takes courage, trust, and self-belief. It also takes *Action*.

The Entrepreneurial Mind-Set of the Level One—The Self-Employed

You see, while the emotional driving force behind most employees is security, those who step into the role of the self-employed are driven by another emotional factor.

This is the desire to be in *control* of their own lives, and of their own destinies.

And, armed with this desire and marching to their theme song, Frank Sinatra's, "I did it *my* way" they're off to create something they never expected.

They're going to create a *job*.

A self-employed person starts out with just one employee—himself or herself. And that suits them fine; no one else to worry about, none of those other people who make all the mistakes; it's just them.

Self-employed people usually trust no one other than themselves to get the jobs done.

They'll say things like: "I am my business." Or, in their sales pitch: "You'll be dealing directly with me and I'm the owner of the business." Or, "If you want something done right, you've got to do it yourself." Or, "Everything is under my control so I know that it's done right."

Remember, most self-employed people started their own businesses because they thought they were so good at what they did, or so good at making what they sell, they mistakenly assumed they could run a business that sells what they make or do.

This mind-set of being the eternally great employee was fantastic when you worked for someone else, but as you'll soon see, it's the fastest way to hard work, and often bankruptcy, as a business owner.

Starting a business where you are an expert at what the business does is usually the first and biggest mistake made by the majority of people going into business.

They start a business in which they know how to make what the business sells, instead of starting, or buying, a business in which they know how to sell what the business makes.

This is the start of the self-employed trap.

If you can do what the business does, and especially if you're the best at it, then it's almost a sure thing you're going to be trapped doing that work forever and a day.

Now, while the trap has already been set, it's this second factor that usually ensures that every self-employed person falls into it.

Not only do they desire control, and think that no one is as good as they are, but *they don't have a vision of "doing" anything else.*

In general, their entire vision is limited by their previous training as a level-zero employee. They've never been trained that when you set up a company, you have to start with the end in mind.

You have to start it knowing that what you're doing is creating something that'll work without you. More about the specifics of this as we go on, but first, let's look at making your vision breakthrough.

What entrepreneurs know that most self-employed have yet to learn is how to envision in their minds and then put on paper what they see as the future of the business.

The self-employed are trapped by the limited "doing" vision that is a part of being an employee. As an example, computer technicians who start their own businesses usually sees themselves servicing peoples' computers and would be extremely happy if they could get enough business to keep themselves, and only themselves, extremely busy.

In other words, most level one self-employed people want to be *busy*. They seem to think that business is spelled—*busy*ness.

Now don't get me wrong. By accident, some will break through this trap all on their own, *but* most are truly set to stay right here until they reach a point of frustration that leads to more than 80 percent of level one self-employed people calling it quits.

They say: "It's not worth all the trouble. I'm going back to get a job and work for someone else."

So, before you make the same mistake, let's examine this vision thing.

When you go into business you need to create a vision that not only sees the business working without you, but one that will inspire and enroll the people who'll be joining your team. You need to be able to see your business as more than just yourself.

You need to see it as a true business, and *not* just as a job for yourself.

You need to create a vision of *your* being more than just a worker in your own business—more than just a manager in your own business. You need to create a vision of a business that works without you—in other words, an investment, your investment.

More about this as we get into the next few levels of entrepreneurs.

The Entrepreneurial Mind-Set of the Level Two—The Manager

Most people who get stuck at the manager level are prone to a set of beliefs about business that is the only thing standing in the way of their success.

First, let's deal with the totally mistaken business belief "bigger is better." For some insane reason it's become a socially accepted belief that the bigger you grow your business the better it will be. Along the same lines, it's thought by some that the way to solve all your business woes is to just get bigger.

How wrong can two assumptions be? It's kind of like motivating idiots; they just do stupid things faster.

Growing bigger when you're running a business that demands your being there all day, every day, is just plain lunacy. If you found it hard to cope with the mistakes and errors when you dealt with 20 customers each day, what do you think you'll inherit with 200 customers per day?

I've seen so many companies grow themselves to death; it's not funny. Growing so fast, robbing Peter to pay Paul, and all the while their mistakes and lack of profitability are covered over by their rate of growth and the extra people they employ.

These companies seem to survive, although no one really knows how or why.

Many then fall into the trap of the second belief—More employees means more success.

Once again this is a completely crazy scenario. So much so I laugh when I hear entrepreneurs bragging about how many people they employ. They seem to think because they pay a huge wages bill each month they must be more successful than the rest of us.

Not so. All this means is rather than turning to a better solution to run their business, they've turned to an older, outdated solution called "hire more people." If only they'd realized business has nothing to do with how many people you employ and everything to do with how much money you make.

That reminds me of another trap—More revenue means more success.

Oh no, this is another beautiful example of ego overriding brain power, logic, and common sense.

Now admittedly your total revenues can determine your company's value, but nowhere near the extent that profits can.

If only they'd realize bigger is not better and stop growing for the sake of growing, they might realize profit is the only score that really counts.

One last belief the level two managers seem to have found for themselves: they truly believe that "Nobody's as good as me."

And what's more, in most cases it's true.

Why? Not because the employees, or as I call them—team members—can't be good, but because the manager is a bad leader.

In most cases, the employees have had bad training, bad goal setting, bad everything, and most importantly, nowhere near enough experience.

Managers hire people they can control rather than people they can lead.

I think it was Henry Ford who said: "The smartest people in the world hire people smarter than themselves."

However, the manager seems to have this firm belief: "If you want the job done right, you've got to do it yourself."

All because they want to be the boss and feel superimportant.

Probably the biggest ego trip of all for level-two managers is that of being the boss. Our level-one friends sang along with Frank Sinatra, yet our level-two buddies have no theme song—just a firm desire to be Bruce Springsteen, The Boss.

They seem to love the power of being in charge more than they love the profits, more than watching others succeed, more than seeing a manual task completed and much more than going home early and trusting other people to do a great job.

Now of course those still stuck at level two will be reading this and feeling ready to kill me, or they will totally refute everything I've said, and with good reason (read: excuses) as to why their situation is different. And yes, it is different, but they now have the choice to change.

By the way, one last belief you'll have to remove if you really want to move and grow: the old "I just can't get good people" belief.

I remember saying this to my dad when I was 21. He replied very bluntly, as he so often did: "Brad, you're getting the people you deserve."

It took me quite some time to calm down and realize what he said was a simple truth. When I started running a great company I got great people, and when I became a great leader, I started running a great company.

I know this all seems so simple, but often the most profound ideas are the simplest. Become a great leader; you'll get great people and they'll run the business for you.

The Entrepreneurial Mind-Set of the Level Three —The Owner/Leader

Owner/leaders experience a massive mind-set shift when they first move up to this level. They operate on an entirely different level than the manager.

Their relationship to the business is entirely different for a start. This brings with it a different way of doing things.

As an owner/leader, one of the first, most important attributes you will have is that you receive passive income. You've reached the position where it doesn't matter whether you get out of bed or not each day. The business can carry on without your having to be there.

You see, you have progressed from working *in* the business to working *on* the business and now you can relax. This might take some getting used to, especially as you're so used to doing things yourself because nobody else could do it as well as you could.

As an owner/leader you're *not* a hands-on person. This means you'll take a more holistic view of the business. You'll be operating at the strategic level and concentrating on the big picture. Your focus is no longer on *cashflow* (others do that now), but on *profit*. The question you'll ask most often is: "Where's the profit?"

The Entrepreneurial Mind-Set of the Level Four—The Investor

Because level four is all about *investing*, or *making money with money* to create *wealth*, you'll be sufficiently removed from the day-to-day running of your business to concentrate on the task at hand.

Operating at this level, you'll want to keep things *simple*. Forget about setting up complicated business structures and reporting relationships. Avoid the temptation of empire building. Your immediate goal is the creation of wealth through buying and selling businesses. That's all. You can, of course, aim to buy and sell many businesses each year. Buy one at a rock-bottom price, build it up, and then sell at a premium price. Use the proceeds from the sale, or some of them at least, to buy investment property and stocks. Read my book *The Real Estate Coach* to find out more about winning the real estate game by establishing property wealth wheels. Do this time and time again, using the knowledge and systems you've learned before.

This brings me to another important concept: *leverage*. You'll be looking to exert as much leverage as you can in your business dealings at this level. If you are going to be building up businesses, chances are you will be using the same or very similar *things* or *services* you will be buying from various suppliers. This is where you will be making use of bulk buying or the loyalty factor to get the best possible prices. You see, what you're ultimately aiming to achieve here is to acquire businesses as cheaply as possible, then to build them up into a salable commodity that has real, intrinsic value, through leverage, so other business owners will want to buy them.

Understand this: Most people looking to buy a business want one that has already been built up by someone else. They want a going concern. They want one that has been set up properly and is making a demonstrable profit. They want to be able to see that all the systems are in place and everything is running smoothly, just as much as they will want to examine the books and financial data.

It may seem obvious, but one of your basic goals when buying these businesses is to get a *good deal*. It doesn't matter in the least whether you happen to like the business you're looking at, or whether it is making a good profit. The deal must be very attractive. It must make good business sense.

And never pay the full asking price—always aim to buy wholesale. If you think about it, why would you contribute towards someone else's profit if you are buying a struggling business—one that isn't doing well at all and about to go under? If it were thriving with good systems in place, then you wouldn't be looking at it in the first place, would you? There'd be little room for improvement and little chance of achieving a dramatically higher price for it when the time comes to sell it. And it wouldn't be contributing towards achieving your business goals and creating wealth.

By now, you'll be having a tremendous amount of fun, buying and selling businesses and building up your own personal wealth. Things will be starting to happen at different paces, different intensities, and different levels. Unless you're careful, you could find yourself drawn back into the thick of things. You could become bogged down and unable to continue finding, buying, and selling businesses. You'll realize that what you need is a *president*.

The Entrepreneurial Mind-Set of the Level Five— The True Entrepreneur

To get to this level, you've got to have learned along the way. You have to have gathered knowledge. You now need to change the way you think. You see, you can't be rich if you don't think like a rich person does. It's that simple. Changing the way you think involves the following four-step process:

- Idealization. Create your ideal world in your mind. Think big. Include everything you ever dreamed of.

- Visualization. Picture that ideal world as if it were real. Do this twice each day, at 10:00 a.m. and again at 10:00 p.m., when you have some quiet time. Spend 10 minutes each session thinking about your ideal world.

- Verbalization. Talk about your ideal world as if it were real.

- Materialization. Things will now start to happen, whether you like it or not. Your ideal world will begin to become a reality. Opportunities will present themselves; you will meet influential people, and your dreams will begin to come true.

The true entrepreneur makes money by raising capital, or to put it another way, by using other people's money to make money.

If the true entrepreneur has a catch phrase, it would surely be this: "Not with my money, you don't."

The true entrepreneur is a visionary, a dreamer of what could be. The true entrepreneur is able to see clearly that which does not yet exist.

The true entrepreneur already has a passive income stream as well as physical assets. The true entrepreneur already has wealth. But what will be achieved at this level is becoming rich through the addition of paper assets.

One other thing: You've probably heard of bulls and bears. How does this relate to the true entrepreneur? It's all about mind-set. Bulls bet the market is going up and bears bet it is going down. But there's one other character I'd like to introduce to you, and that's the pig. Pigs are those people who just have no idea what's going on. They take tips and bet on anything they can, which in reality is nothing more than the leftovers from the real investors. And bear in mind you make money a lot faster as a bear. This is because the market usually drops really fast and climbs relatively slowly.

So there you have it, the business mind-set in a nutshell. How do you shape up? Did you recognize yourself there at all? And did this excite you? If not, perhaps owning your own business isn't for you. If this is the case, then buying a franchise will not be for you either. You see, just because a business is a franchise doesn't mean it comes with some magic formula that will make owning and running it any different to any other business. Just because it comes complete with a set of tried and tested systems doesn't mean you don't have to have a head for business.

A franchise isn't a magic formula to make money. You still need to think like a businessperson thinks; otherwise you'll go to the wall as sure as the sun will rise tomorrow morning.

> "If you're not a risk taker,
> you should get the hell out of business."
>
> *Ray Kroc*

$$\boxed{\textbf{PART 4}}$$

▌Buying a Franchise

Did you know? _____

In Australia, there are approximately 850 franchise systems. During the past two years, one new franchise system has been created every five days. Australian franchising directly creates 163 new jobs every day.

OK, so you've thought about it long and hard, considered all the pros and cons and come to the conclusion that franchising is the way to go. What do you do next? How do you go about finding a franchise that suits your needs and satisfies your longer-term goals?

Where do you start?

The first thing you need to do is to gather as much information as you can about the types of franchising opportunities that are available. To be successful as a business owner—in any line of business—you need to remember one very important thing: avoid buying a business that does what you used to do before you went into business. By this I mean if you are a qualified hairdresser, don't buy a hairdressing salon. If you do, you'll end up doing all the work. It's true. You'll do it because you know that no one you employ could do it better than you can.

This is one of the biggest traps business owners fall into. It traps them into working *in* the business and not *on* it. If they are doing all the work, who's going to be managing the business? Who will be doing the forward planning, the chasing after new business, the marketing campaigns, and the management of team members? I'll tell you who—*nobody*, because you won't have the time. You might try to initially, but after a short while, you'll tire of the long hours you spend toiling away at what will soon become *just another job*. You'll find you won't be able to pay yourself a salary because you'll be required to pay what you make to those who work for you. "Oh, it'll come right in a few months time," you'll tell yourself. "I'll consider it as an investment in my business—then I'll draw enough to make up for it." Sound familiar? Heard other business owners say this? Of course you have. It's something they all say.

But I'll tell you something—it's all rubbish. Absolute garbage. If this is the approach you take, your business will never get off the ground. After a while, you'll either grow totally frustrated at having to slave away in your business for little or no reward, or you'll throw in the towel and go back to being an employee.

And here's another truism. This scenario will be all the more likely if it is your first business venture. That's one reason why I recommend people buy their first few businesses as a franchise because many of these pitfalls have been taken care of. They will, by virtue of their franchise agreement and operations manual, have to spend time working *on* the business even though they might, due to the nature of the franchise, have to work *in* it at the same time.

Even though you might have to *do* the work if you buy a one-man-band franchise (like lawn mowing or dog washing), you'll avoid many of the pitfalls mentioned above because the franchisor will provide you with thorough and comprehensive training. And this will include how to work *in* the business as well as how to work *on* it. And they should have systems in place to ensure you don't stray into the *in* area too much. If they don't, be wary.

So where is the best place to find information about which franchises are for sale? The easiest place to start is by looking through the Businesses for Sale section of your local metropolitan newspaper. There you'll find display ads for major franchises that are for sale at that time. These ads are far larger than normal classified ads and carry much more information. You need to bear in mind that, at this stage, you are still doing your homework and hunting for information of a more general nature. This is precisely what you'll find in display ads.

You'll find information about the franchise system itself, its size, and possibly how long it has been in operation, what they provide, the locality of stores or areas that are for sale, and a bit about the lifestyle you'll have by buying one. The price will seldom be mentioned at this stage. There will always be some kind of invitation to make contact. You see, the aim of these ads is to entice you to find out more.

Isn't that the aim of all ads, you might ask? Well, no, not exactly. Traditional ads aim at getting you to buy something, either by visiting the store or by taking some other form of action. They usually try to persuade you why you should buy that particular product and not the one from the competitor. Price and benefits are major factors in doing this.

With franchising it's different. Sure the master franchisor wants to sell franchises. It is, after all, the ongoing sale of franchises that keeps them in business. But the difference lies in the fact that they don't want to sell a franchise to just anyone. Having the right amount of dollars isn't enough. They need to ensure you meet other important criteria, such as the right attitude and temperament, the right approach to business, and sufficient working capital to see you through start-up. They will want to ensure that you'll fit comfortably within the franchise network and that you will be suitable for that type of business. They will also want to make sure that you will be comfortable working within a system and not branching off doing your own thing.

You should also look at the business classifieds for information, however fleeting, about franchises that are on the market. Here again, don't expect to find out too much—it's just the starting point. But it's in the classifieds that you'll often come across bargain buys. You see, people are only human and they make mistakes. Very often someone buys a franchise only to find out it's not for them. They need to sell the franchise and are prepared to let it go cheaper just to get out. People also become ill or suffer other tragedies that necessitate the sale of their businesses. If you come across one of these, you'll still need to go through a vetting and acceptance process with the franchisor.

Another good source of franchises for sale is the business press. These are specialist magazines that are available at all leading newsstands. Some focus only on businesses for sale, while others focus on business opportunities. There are even specialist franchise magazines, which I recommend you read in any event, because in them you'll be able to quickly assess what the franchise industry is all about and what it's like running many of the more popular franchises. They run in-depth feature articles on many aspects of franchising on a regular basis as well as columns dedicated to answering many of the more common questions and challenges franchise operators have.

These days the Internet plays an important role in our lives and it is here you'll come across lots of important information about franchise systems, what they involve, and how to inquire further. Always check out the site of the major Franchise Association in your country, as you'll find a wealth of unbiased information about different franchise companies. You'll also come across their franchise sites, many of which are linked to the Associations' pages. Check out http://www.franchise.org and http://www.worldfranchisecouncil.org/

These organizations will also be able to supply you with material about what you need to think about when buying a franchise. Read it and digest it.

Then begin narrowing down your search for a suitable franchise by honing in on a selection of systems that appear at first glance to meet your requirements. Obviously you will, at this stage, be making your selection based on what can only be called superficial information, but at least you will be narrowing down the field. You will be able to fairly easily eliminate much on offer just by reading about the type of work that will be involved. For instance, if you see yourself running a retail outlet of some description, you'd be able to rule out lawn-mowing services, cleaning franchises, antenna installation businesses, and business service franchises. Similarly, if you didn't have the better part of a half-million dollars or more to spend, you wouldn't be bothering with fast food outlets or clothing stores.

Once you've done that, the next thing to do is to start gathering more detailed information about them. Begin by checking out their Web sites, visiting their stores or premises (if applicable) and looking at their consumer ads. Aim to get an idea of how the franchisees operate, what they charge, and what sort of service they promise. Talk to customers to gauge public impressions. Try and find out if the franchisor has been involved in any legal issues with franchisees. Your local newspaper office is a good place to start. Their librarian might be able to do a search for you.

Once you've gone through this exercise, you'll probably be able to narrow your selection down even further. You might have decided to scrap one or two from the list.

Now it's time to start making contact.

Call up the contact numbers listed in their ads, and request more information. It's quite likely at this stage that you'll be sent some more information, some of which may be in greater detail than you already have. You might even be asked to fill out some paperwork, which must be returned before you can proceed any further.

By now you will have a very good idea of what system you want to pursue. Your first fact-to-face meeting will not be far away.

This meeting will be a crucial part of your selection process because it will tell you a lot. And here I'm talking about those less obvious, but equally important, factors that are so important when going into business. Things like the corporate culture, the level of confidence and commitment those at management level have in their business, and whether you feel you'll fit in and get along with those who will be your superiors.

You should now be in a position to run with just one of your original selection of systems. You should be feeling comfortable within yourself about what you have gleaned so far and you should be feeling excited at the prospect that very soon you could be running your own business.

It's now time to start the official application process. This will most probably be a fairly lengthy and involved process, and for good reason. You see, you will be being assessed as much as you will be assessing the franchise system. And remember, it's all for your own good. Most franchisors are well aware that too many franchisee failures ultimately damages their business. Word soon gets out and causes not only new prospects to become ultrawary, but existing franchisees become nervous too and begin talking among themselves. This can spiral out of hand very quickly, even if there is no foundation to their fears. And finally, a thorough assessment of your own suitability for the business is in your own interest because mismatches are very costly.

This is the time to reevaluate your financial situation. Make absolutely sure you have sufficient capital at your disposal. You will, by now, have a pretty good idea of what this franchise is going to cost you, as the details will have been discussed at some length during one of your many face-to-face meetings.

Discuss your options with your bank manager, accountant, or any other financial advisers you might have. And be aware that some franchise systems will have vendor financing on offer while others will want to ensure you have *all* the funds readily available. They will not allow you to borrow, even from your own family. Weigh up your options carefully, even if you are offered vendor financing. You see, if the franchisor lends you some or all of the money required to buy into the business, what would happen to you if the franchisor were to get into financial difficulty? Creditors would make a beeline to you and demand that you repay the cash.

And remember you'll need to ensure you have sufficient working capital at your disposal. This is in addition to the purchase price of the franchise. To be on the safe side, work on not earning an income for up to three months. Make sure you budget for your normal living expenses like repaying your mortgage or rent, car expenses, food, clothing, schooling, telephone, entertainment, and electricity. You might want to tighten the belt a little during this period, and that's fine; just be sure to include everything in your budget. And don't forget to include any business-related expenses like royalties, franchise fees, team member salaries, stock, rent, telephone, equipment leases, and insurance. Not all of these may apply to you, but think laterally and draw up an initial start-up phase budget.

Of course, the sooner you are able to get your cashflow running, the better. And having an onerous budget hanging over your head is also a great motivator to make things start happening in your new business sooner rather than later.

One final bit of advice here; keep scrupulous records of absolutely everything. You see, not only will this come in real handy when you get around to filing your tax return, but you can't manage what you can't measure.

Once you've satisfied yourself that you have access to sufficient capital to at least see you through until you've established your business—when it should be bringing in enough money to cover all the running costs—you need to turn your attention to the disclosure documents you will have been given by the franchisor.

In the United States, franchisors are required to provide franchisees with a Uniform Franchise Offering Circular (UFOC). The UFOC is a document that contains information franchisors must provide you by law, designed to assist you in analyzing the merits of your potential franchisor.

There are 23 categories of information that must be provided by the franchisor to the prospective franchisee at least 10 business days prior to the signing of the franchise agreement, including business experience, initial franchise and other fees, franchisee and franchisor obligations, and earning claims.

The UFOC is similar to a securities prospectus. It will provide you with all the information you need to evaluate a company. An accredited franchise company, whether publicly traded or privately owned, must provide this disclosure document.

In Australia, franchisors are required to provide prospective franchisees with a disclosure document. This is a requirement of the mandatory Franchising Code of Practice. The Code was recently amended to extend the purpose of the disclosure document, which is now not only to give prospective franchisees information to help them make reasonably informed decisions about the franchise, but also to give them current information that is essential to running the franchised business. Furthermore, there is now a new requirement for franchisors to continue to maintain a current disclosure documents for a year after they have ceased entering into franchise agreements.

Once you have these documents, read through them thoroughly a few times. Try to understand as much as you can, and place this information in context, bearing in mind your own personal situation. Is there anything that can be "read between the lines," and that can throw more light on the proposition? Is there anything there that, when added to other information you have collected, produces a different perspective on things?

Once you have digested all the information contained in the disclosure document, it's time to consult the experts. Make appointments to see an accountant and lawyer who are fully conversant with franchise matters. If your accountant is only a generalist who isn't too clued in about franchising, find one who is. There are many that specialize in this field.

If everything still stacks up after you have been given professional advice, and if you still feel that fire burning in your belly, then it's time to move on to the final step—the signing of the agreements. And don't forget you still have the protection of the cooling off period. Use this time constructively. Go through all your facts and figures once more. Check everything again to ensure you haven't overlooked anything. Has your situation changed in any way since you first began seriously investigating buying the franchise? Have any external factors changed? What about the state of the economy or the official bank rates? Consider every little factor, no matter how insignificant it may seem at first. Ask yourself "what if" questions. What if you should become ill and hospitalized? What if your car was stolen? What if your house were to burn down? What if your partner should suddenly leave you? How would you cope?

Use this cooling off period wisely. After all, it is there for your own protection. It is a final way out for you should something suddenly change.

Of course, there may be other things you need to consider when buying a franchise. You might need to thoroughly investigate different factors depending on the type of franchise you are after. For instance, if you were chasing a petrol service station deal, you probably would want to look very carefully into the demographics of the area in which the proposed site is situated. Passing traffic, convenience, and local consumer trends and statistics would probably be some of the areas you'd want to look closely at. Retail stores in major shopping centers also have particular considerations like requirements regarding periodic shop-front refits and extended trading hours. What effects do they have on your cashflow predictions?

Brad's Top Tips for Buying a Franchise

- Ask yourself this: "Why am I looking at a business?" Am I looking to just buy myself a job, or do I have the entrepreneurial spirit that running my own business requires? If the thought of buying and running your own business paralyzes you with fear, you need to question whether this is the right option for you. You see, most franchisees that fail do so because they are not suited to the system, and not the other way around. Many of them don't have the entrepreneurial mind-set to run a business; they still have the mind-set of an employee.

- If you could create the perfect business, what would that business be? Then begin looking for franchises that match the general idea you came up with. You see, you must enjoy what you end up doing. You'll find you'll be faced with a huge variety of possibilities from which to choose. Now, choice is a good thing, but too much choice can also be bad in that it can cause you to procrastinate. Let me illustrate it this way: there may be lots of money to be made from running a dog grooming franchise, but if you can't stand animals, it wouldn't be the right thing for you. Sure you'll make money, but you need to be clear on what you want.

- Do your due diligence and speak to a few successful franchisees as well as some who are battling. Ask them these questions: "Why did you get into this business in the first place?" "What have been your greatest challenges and how did you overcome them?" "If you were given the chance again, would you reinvest in the business?" "What suggestions would you have for prospective buyers?" Then ask the franchisor these same questions and see if the answers match. Try to determine what their mind-sets are and compare them to yours. But don't be put off by those that are struggling, if they are in the minority. If they are in the majority, look for another opportunity.

- Develop a business plan and ask some franchisees if they think it's achievable.

- Make sure you go through the legals thoroughly. Spend money consulting with a suitably qualified franchise lawyer. Understand exactly what is expected of you and what the franchisor will do for you. Contact the Law Society and ask them to recommend lawyers with good franchise experience. You see, if you go with an ordinary lawyer, you'll end up paying for hour upon hour of research time required for that lawyer to become suitably acquainted with franchise matters. So spend the extra up front and hire a lawyer with franchise experience; it will be far cheaper in the long run. And don't be afraid to "interview" a short list of lawyers before you settle on one.

- Get a suitably qualified accountant before you take the plunge and sign for the purchase of a franchise. They will help you to structure your future business so that you get maximum tax and financial benefit. Here again, choose one that has franchise experience—and interview them before you choose one.

- Look for a franchise system that meets your needs today as well as in five years. Try to ascertain whether it will grow with you in time. Ask yourself whether it will be viable to branch your franchise out into a business of its own, if that's what you want in the medium to longer term. You see, you might do fine from a lawn-mowing franchise for the first year or so, but should you want to operate another franchise in an adjacent territory, you might find you end up doing all the support work, the maintenance, and marketing for your second franchise, resulting in lower returns from your initial business and a much greater workload. Some franchises are built to develop into bigger, self-sustaining businesses, allowing you to progress to the point where you can receive a passive income. So check this out to see if the franchise fits with your longer-term aspirations.

- Seek the advice of those who know you best—your family and friends. Ask them if they think you'll succeed, then ask them why. This will help you avoid all the emotional stuff that so often gets in the way of making a good, sound decision.

- Ensure that you have the full support of your family, especially if this is your first business venture. Running a franchise will affect your entire family, and they will all have to make adjustments. If you're keen on a retail-type business, you'll probably find you won't have another weekend at home again, which can take some getting used to, especially if you came from the corporate world.

- If at all possible, try to arrange it so you can spend a day with a franchisee. This will give you a better idea of what the day in the life of an average franchisee is like. It'll give you a very good feel for what running the franchise will be like.

- Document everything that is said outside of the agreement. Get as much as you can in writing. You see, franchising is all about relationships, but if you've been promised something that isn't explicitly stated in the agreement, you could end up being very disappointed if the person who made the promise should leave. So get it in writing.

"The number-one business rule is *profit is king*. The success of your business has nothing whatsoever to do with how much revenue it makes or how many people you employ. And it also has nothing to do with what market share it enjoys. It's all about profit."

Brad Sugars

$$\boxed{\textbf{PART 5}}$$

▋ Selling a Franchise

Did you know? _____

VIP Lawnmowing Services started in 1972 and was the first company to franchise lawnmowing in Australia.

VIP now also offers franchise opportunities in home and commercial cleaning as well as window cleaning and mobile car washing and detailing.

_____

Like everything in life, there comes a time when it's appropriate to move on. Nothing lasts forever, as they say. The same is true in business.

There could be a variety of reasons for wanting to move on—for wanting to sell your business. It could be that you have achieved your business goals with this particular business or it could be that a new, more lucrative, opportunity has presented itself. It could also be that you want to move to another city but can't move the business. It could be that you have become tired or bored with the business and can't give it the attention it needs to prosper. Or it could simply be that you just aren't making a success of it and don't know what to do to maximize its earning potential. Perhaps you've realized buying the business was a mistake in the first place and you should never have bought it. Illness and family problems may dictate that you just can't keep going with it and it must be sold.

Every different reason brings with it a different level of *motivation* for selling. And it is this level of motivation that will ultimately dictate what price you are finally able to achieve. You see, if you are desperate and just have to get rid of it at all costs, then chances are astute business buyers will pick up on that and bargain accordingly. If you are in no particular rush and the business is doing fine, then you will probably be willing to sit and wait until you get your price.

You need to be aware of what signals you'll be giving out during the sales process. Think carefully here and don't act on impulse. Plan carefully because, whether you want to believe it or not, your actions will be seen by the market as your next move in this game we call business. Remember that; it's just a game. And games must be fun. So don't get too carried away by making things overly serious for yourself. Now I know selling a business is serious stuff, but don't stress out too much; plan your next few moves as if they were part of a game and you'll find you'll begin sending out positive signals that will be taken more seriously by the market. This will be to your benefit.

Selling a business will generally be one of the biggest decisions you'll ever make. And it will usually be one of the most important. This is because the amount you receive from its sale will generally form a large part of your wealth creation strategy or plans. Your future may depend on its outcome. Your financial viability might depend on it.

So let's spend some time considering the sale of your franchise from this larger financial perspective before getting down to the finer details.

The Big Picture

Understand that to be *rich* you need to have two things that will allow you to produce the third desired outcome. You need a rather large *cashflow* as well as a solid physical *asset* base. These two things combined allow you to create the third part of becoming *rich*, and that's *paper assets*.

Now, I know most people would be happy with being just *wealthy*—you know, lots of *passive* income and lots of physical *assets*. That's fine. And it's easily achievable by buying, building, and selling businesses.

But remember, the only reason you start a business is to sell it.

Generally speaking, you won't become *rich* by owning just one company. You need to buy, build, and sell businesses a few times over. A good strategy is to hang onto your first business for its passive income stream while you acquire and build up your next business. You will be able to do this because you should be aiming at getting your first business to run without you. This is important because it will allow you the time to devote to finding and building your next business. And expect to consider between 50 to 100 businesses before you settle on the next one.

When it comes time to sell your business, you'll need to be a good negotiator. You'll also need to be a good salesperson, but more on that in a while.

You're going to be aiming to get a far higher price for it than anyone else might if they were selling it simply because you'll have finished building it. The buyer just has to move in and start trading. Everything has been built up already. You'll have established the business in your area, it will have a strong and loyal client base, and it will have impressive trading figures. In short, it will present well.

First Things First

The first thing you need to do is to go through your franchise agreement to find out what constraints or limitations you have when selling. Each system is different, and some will set out the price you have to sell for. Others will leave that up to you.

So, what price should you sell for? Are there any broad guidelines that you should follow? Yes, most definitely. Here's what I suggest.

If your franchise it trading well, then set a price based on two-and-a-half to three times its annual turnover. So, for example, if your turnover is $100,000 a year, then set the price somewhere between $250,000 and $300,000. And then add some. If your franchise is losing money, set the price at replacement value. The aim of the game is to get a very good price for your finished business. After all, not only is this now the way you will be making money, but the buyer will be benefiting from all your knowledge, hard work, foresight, and risk taking.

When you think about it, you are selling your dream, right? What's more, you are not just selling a business. You are selling one that actually *works*. The marketing works; the systems work; the people work. Everything works to create the results. This is all guaranteed because you have built a definable relationship here. You will be able to show exactly what is happening in the business—who your customers are, how many times they buy from you, and what the average dollar spent is.

Also, negotiations always begin from the price. Buyers have to start somewhere. They will evaluate your business against the asking price and negotiate from there. Ask too low, and they will still negotiate down from that low price. Remember this; buyers decide based on price, not value.

The next thing you need to do is to consult your franchisor. This is vitally important because, not only do they usually have the right of first refusal, they also need to agree to the eventual purchaser. They may also have a procedure in place that you need to follow. And remember, too, that the franchisor usually has to be consulted every time you alter your selling price because they will, once again, have the right of first refusal.

Once you've taken care of these formalities, it's time to think about advertising your business for sale, using the best medium according to your individual situation. If you need help, call an *Action* Business Coach—they are specialists and can help you design an ad that works. Then it's just a matter of waiting for prospective buyers to make contact.

They'll want to see your operation, and they'll want to go through your books and talk about future potential. They'll then make an offer and expect to negotiate.

At this point, I'd like to remind you about the only reason you got started in the first place. You want to ultimately build up a passive income stream that will give you the ability to become self-sufficient, to become wealthy—to become rich. You have to think of yourself as a business trader, not just a business builder. Got it? You should be aiming to buy, build, and sell, and *not* to buy, build, and hold.

There may well be times when you decide to hold on to a business for a while, and that's fine.

I mentioned earlier that when you sell, you'll be aiming at achieving a higher price for it because you'll have finished building it. What do I mean by that? Well, you've finished building the business when you have achieved your vision for it— when it operates or functions as you originally dreamed it would when you first bought. Basically it is finished when all the systems are in place and operating as designed, allowing the business to run *without* you. And there are very good reasons for finishing a business. First, you will get a high price for it when you sell. Second, because it's now a finished business you can sell it through a broker, who will attract buyers with larger budgets. And third, because the business is producing a passive income stream, you won't be under any pressure to sell. You'll have the luxury of holding it until you get your price.

Some of the things I set up as goals when I start building the business are the following:

- I want to know what my turnover will be on the day I finish building it.

- I want to know what my profit will be on the day I finish building it.

- I want to know what the date will be when I will finish building the business.

- I want to know what the sale price will be on the day I finish building it.

Your business will now be worth considerably more than when you first bought it. You will be aiming to get what it's worth—a very different scenario than when you were considering buying it in the first place.

Understand this: because the profit was built into the *buying* price, not the selling price, you'll be holding out for your price. That's the beauty of it. You will be able to afford to sit tight until the right deal comes along. The business will be running along very nicely without your needing to be there. You can then spend your time sifting through likely businesses to buy next.

Remember my definition of a business. A business is a commercial, profitable enterprise that works without you.

So when is it you can walk away from your business? You can walk away from it as soon as all the systems are up and running and working as they should, and you have a fully trained team in place. The business will now be running itself. If it doesn't, or if snags occur, then you will need to look at fine-tuning some of the systems. Talk to your franchisor, as there may be systems in place to help you do this. You see, franchise systems need to be dynamic; they also need to change with the times. This in itself is a good thing, because it will be testing your systems and people in real-time situations. Once you've ironed out all the teething problems, you should have a foolproof business.

Businesses that run themselves will be attractive to investors precisely because they don't want to become tied down running the show in the first place. That's why they call themselves investors and not sole operators or things like that. The fact that you have developed the business to the point where it can run itself will be very appealing to the investor.

However, it is possible for buyers to come along who intend to run the business themselves. I call this selling to technicians. These buyers are looking to buy themselves jobs, and that's fine if that's what they want.

Vendor Finance

With these buyers, if they are the only ones you get, be prepared to think about offering vendor finance, if your franchisor allows it. Your franchisor may also have the facility available for approved buyers. It may just make the difference between making a sale at a very good price or hoping for a sale and not being sure.

What is vendor finance all about? Vendor finance can be very useful, particularly so if you are asking for a high price. In many instances, a buyer may not have ready access to a very large amount of money, but she might still be the perfect buyer for your business. And it might also be that, for whatever reason, the banks may not be a viable option for her.

Vendor finance often allows for a fast sale, as there are no lengthy delays while the traditional lenders study the finance application in detail.

Very often this is the only way for you to get your price. Buyers may well consider vendor finance as attractive because there may be no interest charges built in. You might offer a straight deal involving a set number of monthly repayments until the purchase price has been met.

Vendor finance also means there may be no capital gains to be taken into account. And the terms of the deal might ensure you keep an income stream from the business flowing that much longer. If the worst came to the worst, you could even state in the contract that, should things not run according to plan, you would get your business back. You would then have earned the monthly repayments along the way as well.

The Most Overlooked Target Market

When selling your franchise, don't forget another very important target market: your existing team (generally known as a management buyout) and employees with a payout. Let's look at them now in a little more detail.

Management buyouts are becoming an increasingly popular way of selling finished businesses. People running and working in a business often see ways of doing things better and making improvements, if only the company were theirs.

Many also dream of owning their own businesses someday, and buying out the businesses that currently employ them means they don't have to leave and get involved with the unknown. They have always wanted to be the boss, and this could be the chance they have been waiting for. There is security in the familiar. Others could fear losing their jobs if someone else buys the business and appoints their own management team to run it. A management buyout could be a way of ensuring job security.

The question you have to ask yourself as a seller in this situation is can they raise the money?

If the business has been built and run properly, it will be producing good profits. Banks might be willing to finance a management buyout, particularly if the bank in question is the business's bank and therefore has a long relationship with it.

Vendor financing is also an option to consider here.

I reckon the best buyer in the world has got to be an employee with a payout. It might be that one of your team members has received a large insurance payout or a retrenchment payout from a previous employer. By buying the business, it could allow employees to just keep on doing things the way they always have. It offers safety and security. And by working in the business themselves, they could save having to pay someone else a wage.

So don't overlook these two useful categories.

The Characteristics of a Good Salesperson

Now let's look at another very important aspect that will have an impact on the eventual price you achieve from the sale of your business—your ability to sell.

That's right, there's no getting away from it; you have to be a good salesperson.

One of the common characteristics of all good salespeople is training. They train continuously. And they keep training. They do this for a number of very good reasons. First, they want to keep up-to-date with the latest trends and techniques. And in today's fast-changing world, this can be a bit of a challenge.

Second, they want to keep motivated. They want their energy levels replenished on a regular basis. One of the best ways of doing this is to rub shoulders with successful salespeople on a regular basis. You see, one of the powerful benefits of doing this is to hear from them what works and what doesn't. It also helps keep you focused on the bigger picture, on what is achievable, and on how you can lift your game by emulating the best in the business. So look out for a sales course and enroll. You won't regret it.

To be successful in selling your business, you need to have strong beliefs. You need to have something you believe to be true. But more particularly, you need to hold a strong set of beliefs about your business, your potential buyers, and the benefits your business will have for them.

You need to understand that, when buyers are making up their minds whether to buy or not, the decision will be based on a mixture of fact and emotion. This is due to our human nature. We can't get away from it. But the important thing you need to know, when faced with a buyer in this situation, is what percentage of the decision will be based on fact, and what percentage on emotion. If you knew that, you'd be in a far better position to help with the process. Of course, this varies according to the type of business being considered, but on average, the decision is a mix of 20 percent logic and 80 percent emotion. How powerful is this to know?

To be successful at selling, you also need to hold strong beliefs about money. What does it mean to you and what role does it play as a motivator? It's pretty important to most salespeople, because their very remuneration package usually hinges on their performance. The more successful they are at selling, the more they earn—it's as simple as that.

Money seems to feature prominently in the life of a salesperson. And so it should. But what is money?

Let me give you my view.

Money is an idea backed by confidence.

Different, huh? That's right. To succeed out there, you need to see things differently. If you don't, you'll be no different from the rest. Understand this: If you see things just as everyone else does, you'll get the same results as they do. And we all know most salespeople don't make a fabulous living.

So let me run this past you once more. *Money is an idea backed by confidence.* Now here's another thing that may come as something of a surprise: The sales process actually starts with *you*. Long before you have a prospect to convert into a customer, and long before you are at the stage of selling your business to a prospect, you only have an idea. You have the idea that you'd like to sell your business to someone. Of course, you have this idea because it's what you want to do. You have already decided to sell your business for whatever reason. But you don't only have an idea. You have something more. You have confidence. That's right. Because you are a confident salesperson, you have confidence in your ability to sell. At this stage, you might not know who you will be selling to, but you'll probably have a vague idea. For instance, if your business is an automotive body works shop, you're probably looking for someone in the trade or someone who already owns a similar business and who is looking at expanding. Now when you combine the idea with the confidence, the end result is money. The money will follow. Get it?

Now if you see money as I do, the way you set out to get it is by harnessing the power of the following four words: Attention, Interest, Desire, and *Action*.

You need to focus your attention on your goals. You then need to have a strong interest in achieving these goals. Mix this with a strong desire to achieve, and you'll be spurred into *Action*. You'll rise to the occasion and perform.

Every salesperson needs to be a good communicator to succeed. Communication is the lifeblood of business, and when it comes to sales, it's vital. It has a direct relationship with sales. You see, the better you are at communicating, the better your sales results will be. You can almost measure the one with the other. Actually, one could be thought of as a barometer for the other. Let me put it another way. True communication is the response you get. So if you're not getting the response you want, you're not communicating properly.

Let's look at this in more detail. Communication, as far as sales is concerned, isn't confined to the words alone. It's far broader than that. In fact, when it comes to communicating, the salesperson has three tools at his disposal: words, voice, and body language. And we use them all simultaneously. The interesting thing, as far as communication in the sales process is concerned, is that words account for only 7 percent of the eventual outcome, the voice is more significant at 38 percent, but by far the most important tool is body language, which weighs in at 55 percent.

Have a good look at these figures.

Remember what I said about your ideas and your confidence? Understand how they influence your body language, and you'll begin to grasp the importance of this in the sales process.

I'm now going to introduce another concept that has to do with communication in the broad sense. It's called Neuro-Linguistic Programming, or NLP for short. NLP is a model of human behavior and communication that draws from the knowledge of psychodynamics and behavioral theories. It is concerned with the identification of both conscious and unconscious patterns in communication and behavior and how they interact in the process of change.

So what does this mean as far as sales are concerned?

If we can understand the three key components of NLP, we can become better communicators. These are:

- Rapport and communication.

- Gathering information.

- Change strategies and interventions.

Rapport and communication cover areas such as language-representational systems, eye-accessing movements, verbal and nonverbal pacing and leading, communication translation skills, and representational system overlapping. These may sound terribly complicated, but the general idea is quite straightforward. If you want to go into them in more detail, there are many excellent books available at most libraries.

Understanding NLP allows us to understand the processes people use to encode and transfer their experience and to guide and modify their behavior. All the information gathering we do is done through three sensory systems: the visual, the auditory, and kinesthetic (feeling and touching). And to a lesser extent, we also use our senses of smell and taste, but these are not of any significance. The really interesting thing here is that visual accounts for 40 percent of the way we communicate, auditory only 20 percent and kinesthetic 40 percent. Isn't that interesting?

So, what does this mean for the salesperson? Well, one of the big lessons here is to learn to match the language system used by your prospect. That way you build rapport very quickly. But be careful not to mimic their language—rather match and mirror the way they communicate.

Successful salespeople also understand the various behavioral styles people have. They understand that people fall into one of four main behavioral groups. They can be either *outgoing* in nature, or *reserved*. Or they can be either *task oriented* or *people oriented*.

Great salespeople have a purpose. Ever noticed that? It's true. Focus on your prospect and you'll always come out in front.

Do you have a purpose? Or have you never really thought about it? Have you always assumed you have a purpose—something like needing to sell your business so you can realize a profit and take on another business to start the whole process over again?

Sit down now and write down your own Purpose Statement. That's right—get it down on paper. Be careful not to confuse your goals with your purpose. Your goals are the more immediate things you are aiming for, like finding three likely prospects for your business, finding one that meets your franchisor's criteria, or being able to make a 25 percent return on your investment. Your purpose is more long term. It touches on the very fundamentals of your existence, on what you want out of life in the broad sense. A purpose could be, for instance, to help people feel good about themselves. You see, such a purpose would involve the notion of caring for others—for your buyers. It shifts the attention away from what *you* want to what your *buyers* want.

Once you have a purpose, start selling on purpose. That's right. Sell on purpose and not by accident, and sell according to the principles of your purpose. Selling according to a fundamental purpose, like the one I've just mentioned, means you'll need to revisit your selling technique. Develop a process that ensures you sell according to the basic fundamentals of your purpose. Here's what I mean:

- Get your prospect's permission before you begin the selling process.

- Begin your selling process by asking a range of questions.

- Offer solutions to your prospect's problems.

- Seek your prospect's agreement before pushing for a decision.

- Explain the investment they are making by purchasing.

- Include a strong call to *Action*.

- Ask their permission to finalize the sale.

You see, what you're going to be doing is running through a questioning process. That's because a problem-solver's best weapon is the humble question. Not only does this help you to find out exactly what your customers want, it's a great way to build rapport. It's also a surefire way of having your prospect do the selling for you. You see, by working your way through a structured, and logical, sequence of questions, you'll find your prospects overcome all the hurdles standing in the way of their decision to buy.

We all, as buyers, go through the same process whereby we investigate various options, eliminating the unsuitable as we go. What we are actually looking for during our encounters with salespeople are reasons why we *shouldn't* buy there and then. That's part of the "shopping around" process. Your job, as a salesperson, is to help the buyer realize (or decide) your business is the one for them.

Remember; ask lots of open-ended questions. They're the ones that start with *who, what, where, when, why* or *how*. Also be specific. Focus on the solutions to their problems, and test their "temperatures" frequently to see if they are getting warmer or colder. Provide detailed answers. One of my Golden Rules to the art of asking great questions is to play dumb and dig deep. Even if you know a lot about your subject, pretend you don't. Ask the obvious and show an interest in your prospects—it will assist them in opening up on an emotional level. And remember, it's on this level that most purchasing decisions will be made.

Use question softeners. These include:

- "Can I just ask ...?"

- "By the way ...?"

- "Incidentally ...?"

There's another important reason you need to ask lots of question. It's a great, nonthreatening way to keep the ball rolling. The key is to ask *lots* of questions.

Develop the habit of listening attentively to what your prospective buyers have to say. It'll make them feel like you have a genuine interest in them. Give out positive strokes. Don't just stand there looking bored, like so many salespeople do. Be enthusiastic, even if they have already intimated that they are going to buy your business. Make sure you understand the question cycle. Question—listen—positive stroke. Make this part of your routine. Get good at it and you'll be amazed at the results you'll achieve.

While asking questions, give out little pieces of information, and talk in the prospective buyer's language.

Depending on the situation or the type of business you're selling, there could be a few more important questions you need to ask. The first has to do with understanding your prospect's authority to arrive at a buying decision. Be sure to ask, "Who other than yourself will be involved in making this decision?" This is particularly relevant when selling a business with a high price tag. Then there's the matter of finances. Ask this question: "Obviously finances are very important. May I ask what budget you've set aside for this purchase?" The answer to this will indicate whether prospects are actually ready to make the buying decision. They may still have to visit the bank to arrange a loan, for instance.

So let's assume now you're at the stage where you can close the sale. You've reached emotion and gathered all the information you need. Ask a question that goes something like this: "Based on what you've told me (prospect's name), it appears this business may well be the solution to your long-term requirements."

When you've suggested it as a possible solution, it's time to check the prospect's temperature with a detailed question. "How does that fit with what you had in mind?"

At this stage, *assume the sale*. Continue with a question something like this: "Would it be OK if I outlined what we need to get the transfer of ownership underway?" Then be silent. Silence here is your greatest asset.

Handling objections is another vital skill you'll need to master if you're going to reap the maximum benefit from buying and selling businesses. It's particularly relevant when selling businesses. You see, selling isn't always plain sailing. Because most prospects will be looking for points of elimination (especially if they're in the early stages of their purchasing process), they'll be raising objections to your arguments. So how do you handle these?

You do so with more questions. Get specific, with questions like these:

- "Is there any other reason besides …?"

- "If (reason) were fixed, would it be OK to go ahead?"

- If the answer is *no*, there must be another reason. "May I ask what it is?"

- If *yes*, "Let's invest some time looking at (reason)."

When it comes to selling, there's another rule you should bear in mind, and that is this: *Persistence pays.* Never forget it. You see, buyers are by nature indecisive. They will be scared of making big decisions and will always want more time to think it over.

There will be instances where, despite your best efforts, the prospect just isn't willing or able to make a decision there and then. In cases like this, most salespeople write them off to experience. But don't give up. Persistence here is the key.

Keep in touch with your prospects. Show them you care. Help them work through the questions that are proving to be sticking points for them. It could be that they still have to reach a decision on whether to buy at all. It may not be your business, or even the price, that is the issue. They may have difficulties with finance or authority that need to be resolved first. Keep close to them and assist wherever possible. Build familiarity and rapport. That way, if they eventually do decide to go ahead, you'll be the first person they approach and not the owner of the other business they were also weighing up.

Make a point of staying in contact over the phone and through the mail. Mail or fax them a brochure or any other pamphlet that you think may be relevant. And be persistent. It usually pays off in the end.

Another key characteristic of successful salespeople is that they are *professional*.

Professionalism is the hallmark of a great salesperson. The more professional you appear, the more your prospect will listen to what you have to say. People like dealing with experts in their field, with someone who knows what they're talking about. They want good advice before buying. They are afraid of being caught by some clever person whose only interest is to make money.

Being professional isn't difficult. All it takes is a genuine desire to help others to reach a buying decision, and paying some attention to detail in the following areas:

- Developing a good sales kit.
- Dressing well.
- Always being on time.
- Keeping in touch with your prospects.
- Preframing your prospect carefully.
- Doing your homework.
- Keeping testimonials.
- Building rapport.
- Finding out what's most important to your prospect.
- Always following up.
- Asking for referrals.
- Sending thank-you cards.
- Being consistent.

Observe these "rules" and you'll outshine the vast majority of salespeople. You'll be one step ahead of them when your prospect comes to making the decision about which business to buy.

You should now have a slightly different perspective about what real *selling* is all about. And it's no different when selling your business. You need to realize that just because it's a business you're selling and not a bar of soap, the rules of good salesmanship still apply. In fact, it's even more important that you observe them because businesses aren't something people buy every day. Making a mistake is far more serious because the effects will live with them for a very long time. If you come across as being thoroughly trustworthy and likable, then your prospective buyer will be all the more likely to believe what you say about how good the business is, what the potential is, and how much opportunity you know there is for growth. It's these intangible factors that can't usually be gleaned from going through the books that very often hold the key to good business buying. Only a good salesperson can sell them to a prospective buyer.

What Else Do You Need to Be Aware Of?

Recent changes to the Franchising Code of Conduct in Australia have abolished the requirement for franchisees selling their franchise to provide a Disclosure Document to the person buying it. But if a master franchisee wishes to grant a subfranchise to a prospective subfranchisee, then both the franchisor and the master franchisee must provide disclosure either separately or jointly. Be sure to find out what laws apply in your country, and seek legal advice whenever there seem to be gray areas.

Brad's Top Tips for Selling a Franchise

- Make sure you actively look for a buyer even though your franchisor might have in place a program to help you exit the system. And check to see exactly what you can do yourself.

- Make sure you have all your accounting up-to-date. You see, prospective buyers will want to see what the financial state of your business is. This is what they will be most interested in.

- Be positive and continue to run the business to the best of your ability. Don't take your eye off the ball just because you have set your heart on selling—it could take you 12 months to find the right buyer, and what will happen during these months if you slacken off? What will happen to your income stream?

- Understand your franchisor's requirements for a replacement franchisee and be very clear on what costs may be involved in selling your franchise.

- Be very clear as to why you want to sell. Ask yourself what you'll be doing next. You see, it may very well be that you are tired and need a rest, but then shouldn't you be taking a vacation? I have had a few franchisees sell up, only to return 12 months later and repurchase a franchise because they hadn't properly thought through the process. After they had sold, they took a long holiday, and then started looking for another franchise. When they realized that they couldn't find anything to compare, they realized they had made a mistake and returned. If they'd just taken some time off, they would have saved a bundle and not had to start all over again.

- You need to understand that prospective buyers will have all the same anxieties as you did when you were in the buying phase. Help them work through it.

"Selling a business is no different than selling any other product or service—the same rules apply. It's just that they usually have a greater number of zeros in the price."

Brad Sugars

PART 6

∎ Franchising Your Business

Did you know? _____

Bakers Delight is the largest bakery franchise in Australasia.

It started as a single bakery in Melbourne back in 1980.

They opened their 600th bakery in November 2002.

_____

The franchise market is a dynamic industry that allows any type of business to grow by distributing products or services. When you expand by selling your trademark and business systems to another person, you adopt the franchise structure. By granting permission as a manufacturer to a distributor or retailer to sell your products, you create the contract of a franchise.

There are many reasons for your wanting to consider franchising as an option for your business. It may be that you simply want to raise a large amount of money quickly to fund future growth or a large research and development project, or you may want to ensure you have more than enough money to retire on one day. Of course, it could be that you really enjoy the challenge of building large and profitable enterprises. It could be that you get a buzz out of leading a large and diverse organization that just happens to be of your own making. Power can be a very important driving force. It places you in control of a unique business entity.

Franchising is an exciting option that allows you to sell your business, over and over again without losing control of the business.

I mentioned earlier that the only real way to *riches* is through buying, building, and selling businesses. Now most that follow this path to financial freedom do so by buying, building, and selling one business at a time. They do one, bank the proceeds, then look for the next, which they then buy, build, and sell. And so they go on.

The *ultimate sale* has to be to franchise the business. You see, when you have developed a sound business that works, it can be duplicated at little or no extra cost. You can sell the business time and time again to different people all over the world. And the beauty of it is there's no limit to the number of times you can sell it.

Think of some of the most popular businesses today, and chances are they're either franchises or they're businesses that operate under licenses. Take McDonalds, for instance. McDonalds is a fast food franchise that operates all over the world today. The potential is enormous, as there could just about be one in every suburb in the world. Each franchisee has a unique territory in which to operate. This ensures the franchisees do not compete with each other.

How to Go About Franchising Your Business

If you run a profitable business and are contemplating franchising, the first thing you need to decide is whether your product range or service is flexible enough to adapt to future trends. The next thing you need to decide is whether you want to franchise your business yourself, or whether you want to call in an expert business to do it for you. I'd recommend the latter for a host of reasons, not the least of which is it's a complex field full of pitfalls and legalities that may not be immediately apparent.

But before you decide on whether to franchise or not, you need to consider whether this route suits you. Ask yourself the following questions:

- Do you see yourself as always striving for excellence?

- Do you possess a leadership style that can supervise and motivate a large number of people?

- Would you enjoy acting as a mentor to a large number of people?

- Are you happy to participate in forums and group activities, which could involve travel away from home?

- Are you happy to invest the money and time to continually learn new knowledge and skills to ensure your franchise system's growth?

- Are you happy to forgo your own way of doing things and follow someone else's systems?

- Are you hungry to grow your business?

- Do you have what it takes?

If you decide franchising is for you, you will need to ensure that your franchise and all documentation and recommendations comply with the Franchising Code of Conduct. Effective disclosure documentation is often the catalyst for a successful franchise. You will need to ensure that you have detailed disclosure documentation to ensure that your franchise model is compliant with the Franchise Consumer Code and provides the potential franchisee a "no secrets" approach to buying the business.

Franchise versus License

So what's the difference then between operating your business as a franchise or licensing it?

Basically, when you sell a franchise, you sell not only a branded business, but also the entire system with which your franchisees can run their businesses in the intended manner. You give them all the training necessary, not only to get them up and running, but also to keep them up-to-date on an ongoing basis. They get all the documentation, all the reporting mechanisms, and all the backing necessary to keep their performance levels in line with what you as the franchise owner demand.

Licensing your business, on the other hand, only gives your licensees the rights to manufacture and/or market a particular product or line of products. How they set up and run your business is up to them. Major pharmaceutical products and cosmetics manufacturers often opt for this method. You see, a license is nothing more than a legal document that gives licensees official permission to do something. They are free to deliberately deviate from normally acceptable rules or practices in carrying out their businesses.

Both options include regular paperwork that needs to be filled in and lodged. And of course, if you are operating as a franchise or a licensed business, you will receive royalties as the owner on a regular basis.

This is what is so attractive about selling your business this way. You get to receive royalties on a regular basis. This is your *cash cow*.

So, what's keeping you? Get your business started and sell.

But there's another very good reason to take your business down the franchise route, and that's a concept called *leverage*. Let me explain.

If you think you can earn more by working a little harder, it's time for a reality check. Take a look around you. Thousands of people you know all work hard, but are they all really getting anywhere? No, of course they're not.

The aim of the game isn't to work harder; it's to create better results with less effort. It's about finding ways of achieving more with less.

You might say the key to success is *laziness*.

This may sound controversial, so let me explain. You need to continually leverage your time, your efforts, your money, and your knowledge.

If you're paid an hourly wage, you'll never earn more than the number of hours you work, but if your business is set up so you're paid whether you work or not, you'll truly understand one of the key principles of success—leverage.

Leverage is simply the ability to do more with less.

Put it this way; employees earn money, business owners make money, and investors and entrepreneurs collect money.

It's all about creating an income stream that flows whether you work or not. And creating one that gets better all the time. Franchising has got to be the ultimate business leverage tool. You see, you can sell your business over and over again, each time collecting fees, royalties, and monthly payments. You do the hard work once when you set up your business for franchising, then the rest just happens. Each time you sell a franchise, you don't have to redo all this setup work; it's already been done. All the systems are in place so the new business owner, the franchisee, just has to follow the system to be in business.

But at this point, let me give you a real-life example of a business that has gone the franchise route.

From Small Pharmacy to International Franchise

Health Information Pharmacy is a retail pharmacy located right next door to a medical center. It is situated away from a shopping center, and it's a stand-alone business with hardly any traffic flow. Many of its customers are middle- to high-income earners, families, some baby boomers, and the elderly.

When Ken and Julia Lee took over the pharmacy in October 1998, it looked tired and was run as a traditional pharmacy—there was very little delegation and the pharmacist did everything. The business needed a good injection of business skills. It also needed merchandising to be introduced.

At college, Ken says he was trained to be a pharmacist, not a business owner. Then once he'd qualified and begun working, he soon realized he needed to accelerate his business knowledge through coaching and mentoring. He also wanted to network with other businesses as a means of helping to improve his own business skills.

After owning the pharmacy for two years, the Lee's moment of truth arrived with the possible deregulation of the pharmaceutical industry and the introduction of discounting. It became apparent that discounting had to be done in volume for the business to survive. But Ken and Julia decided against discounting, opting instead for a policy of adding value. This meant they needed help.

Ken had just read my book *Instant Cashflow* and responded to an advertisement that *Action* Coach Greg Albert had placed in the local newspaper.

When Ken and Julia first approached Greg, their initial goal was to try to free up their time. They were working a 120-hour week between them. They wanted to leverage Julia out of the business first, and then Ken.

One of the challenges they faced was that the business was making a profit while they were working it, but it wouldn't if they stepped out. Obviously they wanted to change this, but they also wanted to create a business model that could be replicated through franchising.

Since teaming up with Greg and *Action*, the business has undergone a complete transformation. They created a business model that proactively takes responsibility for people's health, they developed values that are set in concrete, and they created a unique business around those values.

The core values of Health Information Pharmacy include the following:

- Reducing medication problems.

- Empowerment of people.

- Strengthening their community.

- Helping the less fortunate.

They started by doing an Alignment Consultation and setting goals (which have since changed, but were nevertheless a good start). They then embarked on a program of team training that improved their customer service levels exponentially and developed a team incentive program called Teamaximiser™.

Teamaximiser™ is designed to give incentives to all team members based on their job description. Based on *Action's* "*5 Ways Leverage Chart*," it also encourages companion selling and the giving out of information, while allowing the owner to know what team members are doing every hour of the day. Team members are "penalized" for not following sales scripts or coming to work late.

One of the keys to the success of Teamaximiser™ is that there are bonuses based on individual and team performances; therefore, team members are not just working for themselves but also for a common goal. This is powerful and works well, even without the owners being there. It has also proven highly successful at different sites.

The creation of a Unique Selling Proposition (USP) was also another system that came about through their work with *Action*. Chemconsult™ is now trademarked and is a unique pharmaceutical consulting process. The pharmacy USP fits in with the vision of the pharmacy, which is: "*Advice for a happier, longer and healthier life.*"

Through this system, Health Information Pharmacy is helping to improve patients' lives and keep people out of the hospital. In 2001, there were 140,000 hospital admissions due to medication problems in Ken's hometown. And Ken and Julia believe these problems, to some extent, could have been picked up at the pharmacy level.

Through monitoring at Health Information Pharmacy, it has been shown that one in six prescriptions contain potential medication errors. Chemconsult™ picked up on them and in a large number of cases actually kept people out of the hospital. This not only benefits the patient, but it's also a major benefit to society as a whole.

The Lee's have been able to take responsibility for their business and attack it head-on. This, they say, is one amazing result of business coaching.

The creation of a loyalty club is another system that was developed with the help of *Action*. The Platinum Care Club is the loyalty club exclusive to Health Information Pharmacy, and it offers members more than the normal loyalty club does. Members have access to a 24-hour, seven-day-a week pharmacist hotline and a local area discount book, plus they have free access to a naturopath and a $10 gift voucher for every $150 spent. It is based on a referral system, which has been fantastic for building up the customer base. This fits in well with their core values, which are:

1. Reducing medication problems. This is done through Chemconsult™.

2. Empowerment of people. This is done through the incentive program and management development program in which people are empowered to step up to the next level.

3. Strengthening their community. Unique marketing through Strategic Area Alliances and databases make this possible.

4. Helping the less fortunate. They donate $10 to the customer's favorite charity for every three people they refer to the loyalty club. Most business owners believe they should be donating to charity but don't have a vehicle through which to do so. This is a win-win situation that helps them grow their business while helping needy charities and people at the same time.

Health Information Pharmacy started testing and measuring everything they did. From this they stopped running newspaper ads that didn't work. They tested and measured headlines as well as guarantees. And while some of the guarantees got them into trouble with the Pharmacy Board, because the Pharmacy Act didn't allow them, Ken viewed this as a valuable lesson, as it put them right on track! It also helped them ascertain how far they could go in marketing, yet stay with their core values, as well as the industry guidelines.

Pharmacists were also employed as managers. Systems and Key Performance Indicators were set up to track performances, and Ken's routine changed dramatically. He went from working *in* the business to working *on* it, and now he is working on other people's businesses through franchising. He has also had the ability to create and be creative within the pharmacy setting.

After 3 months, Julia had started to leverage herself out of the business. After 6 months she was totally out. After 12 months Ken was also totally out, although it took another 12 months to franchise the business.

The business outlook is great—the business sees itself as being very community based and as a hub for community activities, especially in the health care arena. There is a naturopath in store. They also have strategic alliances with a chiropractor, massage therapist, gym, restaurant, real estate agent, financial planner, and even holiday destinations.

The business culture is excellent. There is a strong culture within the business and externally as well. The pharmacy has been accepted quite well in the community, especially considering it was one of the first pharmacies to be accredited under quality care, with various press releases and articles being written about the work they are doing.

"The pharmacy was making profit before we took over, but we have doubled the net profit in the last three years," says Ken. Turnover increased by 52 percent (from a large base), profit by 42 percent, and average dollar sale from $30 to $46.

"And although there were not many targets in the early days, Health Information Pharmacy has now been vigorously setting them for the next 12 months. Ideally, the target is domination in the marketplace. We have a strong financial position and a good aggressive group in terms of marketing and pharmaceutical care and how we position ourselves in the market."

However, not everything has been a smooth run. There have been several challenges, which include a car going through the front window of the store one week before accreditation and a landlord who tried to close down the store. Then there were some challenges with the Pharmacy Board regarding some of their marketing strategies.

But the main challenge was discount pharmacies opening in the local area, and in some respects, this is what led Ken and Julia to choose the direction they did. Of course, like every other business, there were also staffing challenges that involved key team members leaving. The positive here is that other team members stepped up and accepted the challenge.

The end result has been huge. There is now a fully systemized business with over 100 systems. A six-volume manual has been created that covers all areas of the business from finance to HR, and from dispensing to management and ownership. This has become a turnkey business for many pharmacists. The owners no longer work in-store, but still know what is happening.

A successful business model based on marketing, merchandising, and team incentives has been developed. Health Information Pharmacy has shown that their systems and models can work in the original store, and they are duplicating them throughout their franchise network.

Ken has taken an office nearby and works purely on developing the franchise. However, he says this is just the beginning for Health Information Pharmacy, as they are now taking the business to the next level—from state to nationwide before going international.

Taking it to the next level is going to be traumatic, as Ken says he will be stepping out of the comfort zone of being a pharmacist once again to leading pharmacists, some of whom have a lot more experience in the industry than he does. "But I am looking forward to the challenge of making a difference in multiple areas," he says. "We will be sharing our values and beliefs throughout the pharmaceutical industry, and it's going to help patients."

And what of the future?

"It has been an exciting time with my business coach. I'm looking forward to big things in the future. He is still involved as my coach, some two-and-a-half years on, and he is also now the Business Development Manager at Health Information Pharmacy. One thing we have insisted on is that as each franchisee comes on board, they get a business coach for at least three months to ensure their success. I would recommend this as a must for any franchise out there. Working with *Action* has been incredible for the business. Every business owner should take it up because it is an investment in his or her own knowledge and skill development."

The Structure You've Got to Use

If you're going to franchise your business, then there's one structure you've simply got to use. You see, if you can't make at least a few million from this, you'll have to kick yourself; it's that easy.

The structure I'm now going to tell you about works extremely well and it's simple. That's the beauty of it. I became a trendsetter using this system. This is how it works:

You franchise your business, not to a myriad of franchisees but to a handful of master franchisees, who in turn franchise business to franchisees in their territory. In my case, I first sold master franchises for the various states to master licensees, who in turn sold franchises to franchisees in their states. These franchisees, who became primary franchisees, are able to, in turn, bring on associate franchises. This enables them to develop a passive income stream from their businesses.

In effect you are setting up a structure that is multilayered.

In the United States, master franchises were sold along state lines, but in overseas markets, I sold master franchises for each country I expanded into. This way, I don't really get too involved in the nitty-gritty of running the business in these areas; my master licensees (as they are known) are responsible for the smooth running of the business in their territories. It is up to them to do everything from selling franchises to supporting the franchisees. Head Office provides training and ongoing strategic assistance, direction, and global communication.

Brad's Top Tips for Franchising a Business

- Make sure your concept has been thoroughly tested to make certain all the systems work and that the business is running smoothly and profitably. Will it stand the test of time or become another business statistic? This is best done by running a pilot successfully first.

- Make certain the business lends itself to being duplicated and that a demand exists for your product or service. Make certain too that your brand is recognized in the marketplace.

- Consult your lawyer, financial advisor (both of whom must have franchise experience), and a franchise consultant. Make sure you have all your legals in place before you franchise the business.

- Produce a set of comprehensive operational manuals, and test to see that they are understandable and that they work. Make sure your manuals take a step-by-step approach and don't assume your franchisees know anything. Put absolutely everything down in the manuals.

- Have an experienced franchise solicitor draw up your franchise agreements.

- Make sure you have enough cash in your budget to sustain the business at least through the first three years, or until you begin to see profits flowing through the system.

- Design your training and support systems system very well. Seek professional help if necessary. Have them in place before you begin franchising—you can't build these as you go because then your first few franchisees will think they are the guinea pigs. Understand that it is the systems that they are actually buying, so if you don't have tried-and-tested systems in place, what are you selling?

- Think carefully about how you are going to select who you sell your franchises to. How are you going to determine who is suitable and who is not? This is most important as the results and experiences of your first few franchisees will determine the longer-term success of your business. If they fail, chances are so will your business, but if they are a roaring success, your business will flourish. So think carefully about this: Are you chasing money so you can expand your business rapidly, or are you looking for certain qualities in your franchisees? If so, what are they? Remember, these people will set the ball rolling for you.

- Design marketing and PR systems that are above reproach. They must be as professional as possible.

- Give a lot of thought to how you are going to cultivate your relationships with your franchisees so they can remain as cordial as they possibly can. Much is going to depend on this, and if your system is lacking here, it is going to severely test you in the years to come. Keep your lines of communication as open as possible.

- How are you going to ensure that your franchisees are able to remain at the forefront of their market? What provisions have you to ensure that your research and development is as good as it can be? And will this be good enough?

- Do you understand The Franchising Code of Conduct? It is mandatory in Australia. Be sure to consult the laws in your country.

- Make sure you have a detailed and up-to-date folder on every franchisee in your system. Keep everything documented. You see, franchising involves relationships, and these relationships are both personal and legal. And they come unstuck every now and then. So document everything, not to trap anyone, but rather to cover yourself should you end up in court. Include sign-offs in your system so franchisees can sign that they are happy with things as they work their way through the system. For instance, on completion of initial training, get them to sign a form stating they are satisfied with the quality of training received. Be in a good position to put forward your case, if required to.

- Learn as much as you can about the anxieties franchisees face before they purchase a franchise, when they make the purchase, and as they work as a franchisee.

- Make certain your system is adaptable and able to take on board suggestions and experiences from your franchisee base. Remember, a franchise system is just like a tree; it's either growing or it's dying. It simply can't stay the way it is *ad infinitum*.

The bottom line here is you need to be well prepared before taking your business down the franchise path. If you're not, you could end up fighting lengthy and costly legal battles. Nobody wants these and besides, if your business fails, it will be precisely the opposite result of what you were hoping to achieve in the first place.

Failure is not part of the plan. If this is where your franchise hopes end, you'll have to seriously question whether you planned to fail, or failed to plan.

Common Mistakes

It is a good thing to at least *think* about failure before you get underway with the franchising of your business. You see, if you knew the main reasons why many franchise operations fail, do you think that could help you not to make the same mistakes? Do you think you could plan early so you have systems in place to ensure the chances of your making the same mistakes are minimized? You bet.

So what are the most common mistakes franchisors make?

Probably the most well publicized is greed. What many of them seem to want is quick cash. The greed factor has led to many spectacular crashes in recent times that have left a trail of bitter, disappointed and broke franchisees who have lost everything. These highly publicized disasters have given franchising a bad name, but fortunately things are getting better; the authorities have introduced legislation to regulate the industry, and the industry itself has developed a far more responsible attitude towards business in recent times.

The next reason some franchisors fail is due to poor selection techniques when selling franchises. This is probably related to the greed factor because all some franchisors are interested in is selling franchises. They are only interested in their own cashflow situation. Selling franchises is fine, but for the long-term sustainability of the system, it pays to be very selective when choosing whom to sell franchises to. You see, get this wrong and you'll end up with disgruntled franchisees beginning to quit simply because it wasn't for them. It wasn't their cup of tea. And disgruntled franchisees start talking to others and saying things tinged with emotion and bad feeling. It does your business no good at all because word can spread like wildfire. Other franchisees who might be "sitting on the fence" or going through a rough patch might get caught up in this and talk themselves into failure. You need to bear in mind that, in franchising, the situation can develop rightly or wrongly into "it's you against them"—the franchisor against the franchisees. This is just a fact of the business, because the two entities really do have different aims and ambitions, even though their overall goal would be the same. You can think of it much the same as the classic boss-worker analogy.

Franchises fail due to insufficient or poor training. They aren't sufficiently equipped to tackle what lies in store for them. They return from initial training knowing no better, but pumped up with enthusiasm. They are ready to make their mark on the business world, but when situations arise that they are ill-prepared to take on, they begin to feel incompetent and inferior. Only this time they have no one to turn to, because they will by now be having doubts about you, the franchisor. You see, if you let them down by not training them properly, what else will you be neglecting to do? Will you be able to satisfactorily assist them with day-to-day operational matters? You will have lost their trust and confidence, and from then on, it's usually just a matter of time before you lose them altogether.

The stagnation of new product research and development is also a major reason some franchise systems fail. It might be all well and good when the business is initially franchised, but as time goes by, the business environment will change and your business must keep pace with changing times. You must equip your franchisees with the tools necessary to compete in the marketplace. You must help them to stay competitive and in business.

Some franchises make such rapid inroads when they first appear that the owners begin to believe their system is so good they can expand at a meteoric pace indefinitely. The simple truth is few can. Growing too quickly can be the downfall of even the best franchise system in the world. It's like any business that's growing too quickly—the first problem they'll experience is a cashflow shortage. That's right, even though they have customers pouring in through the doors, they will find their cash beginning to dry up, because they'll be purchasing stock and investing in enlarging their facilities so they can handle the extra demand, all of which costs money, yet profit takes time to work its way down through the system and into their coffers. I know this may seem like a contradiction in terms, but it's true. Growing too quickly can be really disastrous.

Franchisors that fail to continuously test and measure the performance of their franchisees often only realize there is a problem when it's too late. The secret is to have systems in place that measure their performances on a regular, ongoing basis.

That way all that is needed is a small tweaking here and there to keep them on track. It's often more efficient and less painful to make a series of small corrections than one large one. It's also less costly.

The final reason some franchise systems fail is that they don't pay nearly enough attention to developing meaningful relationships with their franchisees. This results in a breakdown of communications in the true sense of the word; there isn't nearly as much openness and trust in the business between the various players, leading to conflict. Conflict, when not handled properly or resolved, only ends up in litigation, which no one really wants.

The Secret of One Franchisor's Success

Let's look now at what the secret has been for one of the world's top franchises—Subway. "The appeal of a Subway franchise is universal—with low investment, a simple operation, and unparalleled support for the franchisees," says Don Fertman, Subway's Director of Franchise Sales. And according to the franchise's president and cofounder Fred DeLuca, "We have a very simple approach to business. What's really great about our team is that they keep analyzing the market; they do a lot of research and testing and stay focused for the benefit of all our franchise owners."

> "To succeed as a franchisor, it's imperative that you remain responsive to new ideas."
>
> *Brad Sugars*

$$\boxed{\textbf{PART 7}}$$

■ Franchising—A Question of Relationships

Did you know? _____

Subway Restaurants, the franchised chain of sandwich shops, has eclipsed McDonald's as the largest restaurant chain in the United States.

The chain operates 13,247 stores in the United States, 148 more than McDonald's.

Subway, started by Fred DeLuca in 1965, now has over 24,000 restaurants around the world.

_____

Franchising is really all about relationships. This is what it all boils down to. Make sure you develop great, lasting relationships and you will be giving yourself every chance of making a success of your franchise business.

But let's go into this a little deeper.

The first thing you need to think about is what your motive was for buying a franchise. Or if you haven't bought it yet, why are you thinking of buying one in the first place?

Understand this, and you'll be on the right path when it comes to deciding how you can approach this issue of relationships. Get this clear in your mind and you'll have a clearer picture of the role relationships play in the world of franchising.

Why would you want to go into business for yourself? Just look at the statistics. Around 80 percent of businesses started this year will be gone in five years.

Most business owners seem to work harder than any of their people and many seem to earn less than they could make elsewhere.

From what I've found, people start their own businesses for one thing and one thing only: *freedom*. Whether that is working for themselves, having more time to themselves, financial freedom, or just the freedom of knowing that they're in charge.

They have a longing to be in charge. They want to "do it their way." They want to be responsible for their own destiny. Now all this is absolutely fine; it's fantastic and it's positive, but it's not going to just happen for you because you have made this great, big, important decision. Your life won't miraculously change the way you want it to.

Traveling down the road of life, it's easy to be distracted, to get off track and lose sight of the big picture. What's the old saying? "Can't see the forest for the trees." However, every day you're getting little taps on the shoulder, an idea that you should change what you're doing, a suggestion from someone, a hint, and you either learn to take the taps, or eventually they become signposts you run into.

And the signposts are a whole lot bigger and they hurt a whole lot more. Then if you're still too blind, too stubborn, or just too stupid to read the signs, you'll stray into the path of oncoming traffic and get run over by the proverbial Mack truck.

Why do you think that most successful people are great networkers? Why do they seem to have great relationships with friends and colleagues? It's because they've perfected the craft of surrounding themselves with other people and then listening—*really* listening—to what they have to say. They have developed these relationships to the point that they have *earned* the right to ask others for advice. They can in one night absorb more "taps on the shoulder" than many take on board in a whole year. Just remember to get the facts, listen for the taps, and look for the signs. Sticking your head in the sand never helped anyone.

When you think about it, you can't survive in business without paying particular attention to the relationships you have with others. It's like the lifeblood of business. You need to understand that, whether you like it or not, you *will* have relationships with a whole range of people. You see, if you dislike the idea and believe you are the shy type who prefers to get on with things alone, then the relationships you have with others will be cold and aloof. You will come across as unfriendly and uncooperative. Relationships are something you can't avoid. They develop whether you like it or not. And here's another thing to consider: Relationships can be worked on so that they take the shape and form you want them to take. And it takes just as much effort to develop good relationships with others as it does to develop bad ones. It costs nothing to smile at someone, to be friendly and polite. The choice is yours. It all depends really on how successful you want to be in business.

When it comes to examining the types of relationships a business has, it is convenient to categorize them into two distinct groups: external relationships and internal relationships. Let's look at them separately.

External Relationships

The very basic form of relationship any business develops is with those who deal with it. And the first manifestation of it is through another well-known, but often poorly implemented concept: customer service. You see, it's through the service you give to your customers that they begin to form their first impressions of you or your business. And it's these impressions that drive your relationships with them.

So let's look a little closer at the concept of customer service. Let's take it one word at a time.

Who Is "The Customer?"

So who then is your customer?

If you really begin to think about it, there are four classes, or types, of customers and they're all equally important to you. Who are they? They include:

- The Owners: Business must serve them by providing an acceptable level of profit.

- The Team: Business must serve them by providing recognition, rewards, and a paycheck.

- The Suppliers: Business must serve them by paying their bills.

- The Customers: Business must serve them by meeting their needs.

As you can see, customers are a diverse group of people that come from all walks of life. They also have various, and differing, relationships with the business. They do have one thing in common, however. They all have needs and wants.

The needs and wants of the owners will be different than those of the team, and suppliers will certainly have different needs and wants than those who buy from the business. But they all have needs and wants. It's the job of the business to discover what those are, and then to sell them what they need.

Of course, they will be selling rather differently to owners of the business than they would to suppliers. Selling takes place on different levels. The team has to be "sold" on the business; otherwise they'd leave and look for better employment, if they didn't believe the business had a future. Owners could sell their shares if they weren't "sold" on the business's outlook by the management team. And suppliers wouldn't offer generous credit terms or prices if the business wasn't "sold" to them correctly at the outset.

You need to understand that providing great customer service is all about relationship building—and this means communication.

It's a two-way street that involves an Emotional Bank Account in which you make deposits and withdrawals. You need to establish your Emotional Bank Account with your customers by first making a deposit, much as you would an ordinary bank account. You would, for instance, make a deposit of trust, goodwill, price incentives, or the offer of a good job. Then, after you have built up a positive account through showing your customers you are genuinely interested in their needs and wants, you can begin making withdrawals. You can, only then, begin expecting your customers to begin assisting you to achieve your own goals, helping you reach your sales targets, referring friends, or becoming Raving Fans.

Who Is Your Ideal Customer?

It's often said there are customers, and there are customers. How true this is.

There are those customers you'd love to deal with every day, and there are those you wish would never come back. But there are more than just two basic groups. There are, in fact, four categories: A, B, C, and D. I explain them as follows:

- *Awesome*

- *Basic*

- *Can't deal with*

- *Dead*

You might wish to only deal with the A's and B's. If that's the case, get rid of the rest. How do you do that? Simple. Tell them. Or set up rules for doing business, then write to everyone on your database, explaining you're repositioning your business and here are the new rules. You can also change your pricing policy or the décor of your premises—this alone will filter out those you don't want. A video store wanted to shake off the young hooligans who had taken to gathering there. All they did was change the type of music they played in the store. Instead of playing music teenagers listen to, they began playing classical music. Their client base changed virtually overnight.

If you were to really analyze your business, you'll find that 20 percent of your customers account for 80 percent of your business. This is what I call, the 80-20 Rule. Do you know who your 20 percent is? These are the ones you should be concentrating your efforts on.

Satisfaction

Now that we've looked at the first word in "Customer Service," let's look at what lies behind the second. Begin by asking yourself this: Do customers leave your business feeling satisfied or delighted?

I know this is a profound question, but you do need to give it some thought. Be honest with yourself. How do your customers really feel about doing business with you?

The first thing you need to understand is that customers *expect* to be satisfied when making contact with any business. They have a need they want satisfied. They've also gone to the trouble of finding out which businesses can satisfy their need, then they've done something about it—they've either phoned up or actually traveled to your business. What happens next will determine the lasting impression they have of your business.

They *expect* satisfaction, but will actually talk to others about your business if they get more than they *expect*.

So give them something to talk about.

This is the first step in creating great relationships with them that will result in their becoming what I call Raving Fans.

Good Customer Service is proactive. Don't wait until you have a problem in this area before doing something about it—before you think about ways and means of taking care of your customers. How can you give your customers something more than they expect?

Think of different things you could do to get them talking. Brainstorm. Consult your salespeople. Start becoming innovative in this area. Think outside the square.

Make this part of your routine. Get used to constantly searching for new ways of satisfying your customers. Keep your eyes open, watch what other businesses are doing, and keep innovating. You see, customers actually *expect* you to keep getting better.

Moments of Truth

Do you know what your moments of truth are? They are the times when it really counts to impress someone with your service.

Do you now know what yours might be? Take the time now to list as many of them as you can. Be ruthless with yourself. A good place to start is with your customer interaction.

Once you've jotted down some of your moments of truth, you'll begin to see why customers leave you for a competitor. You'll begin to develop ideas to stop this in its tracks.

Before we go any further, here are some statistics about why customers leave that may startle you. They are:

- 1 percent due to death.

- 3 percent due to a house move.

- 5 percent due to buying from a friend.

- 9 percent due to buying from a competitor.

- 14 percent due to finding a better product or price.

- 68 percent due to perceived indifference.

These figures are staggering. Sixty-eight percent of your customers leave because they perceive your business to be indifferent to their needs. They feel you just don't care.

Now look at how many leave because of the efforts of your opposition. The figures are so small as to be almost negligible. Only 9 percent are swayed by the active efforts of your competitors, while a mere 14 percent find a more attractive deal elsewhere.

Remember my 80-20 Rule? If you were to really do well with only 20 percent of your customers, you'd be looking after those that account for 80 percent of your revenue. So how hard is it to hang on to that 68 percent slice of customers who leave just because they think you don't care about them? Putting this another way, how easy would it be to retain that 20 percent of customers who contribute the most to your bottom line just by treating them decently? Why do all the difficult (and costly) things to shore up your bottom line when a simple remedy like offering great customer service can do it for you?

Winning Customer Service

OK, so you've decided the level of service your business provides its customers could be a whole lot better. What do you do about it to make it the talk of the town?

Let me now share with you the three steps you must take to achieving great, and meaningful, customer service.

Step 1. You must aim for *consistency*. It's no good if whatever you do differs each day. Your customers will want to know that whenever they visit your business the service will be the same. And it doesn't matter what the level of customer service is, so long as it's consistent. I mean if you are running a five-star hotel, you will serve your dinner guests at their tables, whereas if you were running a fast food outlet you wouldn't. This doesn't mean the customer service at the fast food joint is inferior to that at the hotel. It would just be different, at a different level. And you must offer consistency in both service and delivery.

Step 2. Make it *easy* for customers *to buy*. You see, with consistency comes *trust*. By building consistency into your sales process, you will ensure that you systematically surpass their expectations every time they buy from you. They will begin to trust your business; they will know every time they buy from you there will be no unpleasant surprises. They receive the same pleasant greeting each and every time they arrive, they receive the same efficient and courteous service while they are there, and their questions are answered accurately and honestly. Do everything possible to make their buying experience easy. This way, they will know what to expect when they return next time.

Step 3. Now introduce the *wow* factor. This is the way to create Raving Fans. Understand this: The fundamentals of creating great customer service involve creating a system to make sure your customer's expectations are surpassed, every time. Having satisfied customers implies you have given them all they've wanted, and nothing more. But if you're going to surpass their expectations, you must systematically go beyond their expectations. Every single day you need to be getting better. The Japanese have a good term for this. They call it *Kaizen*— constant and never-ending improvement.

To do this, you need to go further than just providing great customer service. You need to implement a customer service plan, which includes the following action points:

- Identify your ideal customers. Find out who they are.

- Create your customer service vision. Remember, customer service is about understanding that little things are important. You need to make an impression on your customers.

- Conduct market research. You need to ask your ideal customers what they would regard as excellent customer service.

- Now create your customers' customer service vision.

- Take the two visions and combine them to create an ultimate customer service vision.

- Decide what it is you can promise your customers. This must be something you can deliver each and every time. My rule is to underpromise and overdeliver.

- Make sure you get your team involved. Give them the vision, and ask them for ideas on how it can be delivered. Work consistently with them on this.

- Make sure you have continual checkups. Make sure you are delivering what you promise.

- As your level of service gets better, move the goalposts. Keep improving.

- Always give your customers more than they expect. I send out free gifts continually.

- And always smile. You see, people love to feel special.

People are willing to *pay* for service—when it's the service they desire. If the service exceeds their expectations, they will *stay* with you and they will *say* good things about your business.

But if your service is poor, they'll *walk* away, they'll *talk* negatively about your business, and they'll *balk* at coming back.

Be consistent, always smile, and give your customer's more than they expect. That way you can be sure they'll leave with smiles on their faces.

The Ladder of Loyalty

Most good businesses spend time and money in the pursuit of good customer service so they can get customers to come back and make further purchases. But understand that good customer service in itself doesn't build customer loyalty. Take, as an example, two businesses. One gives average customer service and the other prides itself on its good customer service. If the first business writes a follow-up letter to its customers inviting them to shop there again, whereas the second one doesn't, where do you think the customers are more likely to shop next? At the first business, even though its customer service is rated as only being average.

OK, so let's take a closer look at this very important concept—customer loyalty.

How do you build loyal customers? I like to explain this using the Loyalty Ladder concept. What I mean by this is you have to move your customers up this ladder, and you need to keep them moving up the ladder all the time.

Think of it just like an ordinary ladder. If you were to step up onto the first rung of the ladder, would you just hang around there for a while before doing something? No, you would want to climb up right away, or get off.

Now, ask yourself why it is you want to build a Loyalty Ladder for your business. I'd suggest it is because the first sale you make to a customer is made at a loss. Yes, statistics show that 9 out of 10 first sales are made at a loss, because there are advertising costs, marketing costs, and commissions that first need to be taken into account. If you don't get that customer to come back and buy again, that customer isn't profitable to you.

Let's now take a closer look at the Loyalty Ladder and what the various stages on it involve:

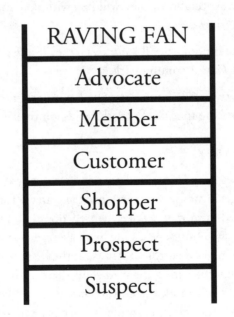

RAVING FAN
Advocate
Member
Customer
Shopper
Prospect
Suspect

1. **SUSPECT.** When they first start out on the Loyalty Ladder, right at the bottom rung, people are called suspects. How do you identify them? They are only potential customers at this stage; they fit within your target market and they are willing to buy from you if they are in your geographic area.

2. **PROSPECT.** We then move up the ladder to prospects. Prospects are suspects who have taken some sort of action like phoning from an ad or visiting your business. You must collect all their details so you can stay in touch. This is most important, as building customer loyalty is all about relationship building. You will be aiming to build a database of prospects. You now use all your sales skills to move your prospect one rung up the ladder to the next stage, to that of customer.

3. **CUSTOMER.** To be classified as a customer, your prospect needs to have spent money, and you need to have recorded the sale in your records. This last step may seem strange, but it is most important because it allows you to differentiate between prospects and customers on your database. You see, if you are planning to send a letter out to all prospects offering them an incentive to buy, you don't want to be sending it to people who are already customers. This record will also tell you when they last bought, how often they buy, and what their average dollar sale is. Here's something you'll find interesting: I find most businesses put up a huge *stop* sign at this level. The salespeople seem to sit back waiting for these customers to return, instead of taking proactive action and inviting them back. Understand that at the customer level, they have cost you money. If you are content to stop at this level, your business will eventually go broke. I have eaten out at many restaurants, and guess what? I'm not on any database. I've never received a letter from any of them saying: "Brad, we'd love to have you back." This is, to my mind, quite insane. They seem to be saying; "You've bought, now I'm going to just hope like heck you come back." Think about the possibilities for your business. The *stop* sign is the scariest thing I've come across in business. You need to get rid of it, and fast.

4. **MEMBER.** When your customers make their second purchase, they become members. They now have a feeling of belonging. Understand that customers who make two purchases are 10 times more likely to make more purchases than someone who has only made one. So, you need to put some effort into your members. Give them a membership card and a membership pack. How many of your customers know all your products? Very few, I would suggest. So why not include a product catalog in the membership pack? You can also include samples, vouchers,

and things like that. One interesting example I came across recently was at a truck stop in New Zealand. The owner pinned up photographs on a notice board of all drivers who had stopped the night there. Then there's the coffee shop that gives you your own personalized coffee mug. Each time you come in, they get your mug down from the shelf for you. These two examples give members a sense of belonging.

5. **ADVOCATE.** Once you have members, you move them up the ladder to the next level—to that of advocate. An advocate is someone who sells you to other people. The criteria for advocates are they will give referrals or promote you, and they keep buying. Advocates are one of your major capital assets.

6. **RAVING FAN.** Once you have created an advocate, you need to move them up to the top of the ladder where they become raving fans. Understand the difference: An advocate is someone who will sell for you, whereas a raving fan is someone who can't stop selling for you. The exciting thing about Raving Fans is they can almost be regarded as part of your team. They want to see you succeed. Of course, they continue buying from you all along.

Remember, the aim of the game is to move people up from Customer to Raving Fan. This is where you begin to make profit. And remember, people are prepared to *pay* for service.

We have now looked at your external relationships in some detail, but this is just one aspect of the relationships you will need to concentrate on. You also have internal relationships that are just as important. You see, the way you interact with your internal stakeholders, your staff, and your franchisor is just as important as your relationship with your external stakeholders, your customers.

Internal Relationships

Many businesspeople have the misguided impression that just because what goes on inside their business isn't visible to the public, it is not important and of no concern to anyone other than those who work there. What rubbish.

This is where many go wrong. The way you get along with the members of your team is vitally important to the well-being of your business. It's just like the importance of having a healthy heart. Just because it's inside you and can't be seen doesn't mean it can be ignored. Let's look now at some of the important things you need to consider to ensure that you establish internal relationships that are conducive to the development of a healthy, vibrant business.

Culture

To begin with, one of the most important strategic moves you can make when buying or establishing a new business is to think about the culture you'd like your business to adopt. Ask all your team members to contribute, as this allows them to buy in and identify with the business in a fundamental way. After all, they are the ones that will be the life and soul of the business on a day-to-day basis. They need to feel comfortable working there and they need to be happy with their working environment.

Once you have reached a consensus on this, write it down and display it prominently at key locations in your workplace.

Remember, your company's culture starts with you. You set the tone and the standards. This was one of the very first things I did when I established *Action International*. I had my team come up with what we call our 14 Points of Culture. Everyone adheres to them, and they are explained to all prospective team members when we hold our interviews. That way they know the environment they will be hoping to join and the culture they will be fitting into.

We also hold all our interview sessions as group sessions where all members of our team participate together in group interviews, which take the form of a deselection process. You see, we believe that because we pride ourselves in having *fantastic* internal relationships, every team member has an equal say in who comes to work here. They all have to, after all, get along with new additions to our team. We also interview all aspiring team members *together* in a group, so that we all can weigh up the different personality types in an effective way. We spend the first half of the interview session outlining what our company does and what our goals and mission are. We also explain in detail what our 14 Points of Culture are.

Then members of the team have a chance to outline their roles within the company and what their experiences have been working for the company. They also talk about how the team fits together and how they work together, both in busy times and in times when things are a little more relaxed. They talk about the good and the bad in an unthreatening atmosphere.

Then after a short break, the interviewees are asked to answer three basic questions, one person at a time. This is done in the group situation so that every interviewee can listen to what the others say. Some find it intimidating, as they aren't used to being open, and others are put out, as they aren't used to talking in front of a large group of strangers. This is part of our deselection process and we make it clear that anyone can slide out at any time should they feel they won't fit in. The end result is we always end up with fantastic people working for the company, people who share common beliefs and outlooks and who are prepared to work together to achieve common goals. Another result of this process is that all our team members feel they can, from the moment they join, work in an open environment where real, effective two-way communication is encouraged. Nobody has anything to hide and can feel free to ask for help or discuss challenges or concerns before they become major stumbling blocks.

This culture of openness is further encouraged through our weekly WIFLE sessions that take place every Friday afternoon. The idea is that everybody gets a turn to speak to the group in an uninterrupted and open forum, free from the threat of reprisals or repercussions. WIFLE stands for *What I Feel Like Expressing*. This is the forum for getting things off your chest or for expressing thanks for help received. What is said in session stays there and is not spoken about again afterwards. The sessions end by everyone 'Whooshing" it away for good.

Now that's a look at our culture. Of course, every company will have a different culture and that's fine. As long as it reflects the collective feelings, likes and dislikes, and ways of going about business, that's OK.

Every business will have a culture. It's just that some cultures develop all on their own because nobody takes charge and directs the way it comes about. And chances are, these haphazard cultures don't do anything positive for the business. They usually just evolve as time goes by, incorporating many counterproductive elements like a propensity for gossip, for office politics to become a dominant factor, or for bullying to rule the roost.

The scary thing about company culture is that once established it's extremely difficult to change. Usually the only way to effect a change is by getting rid of your team (or most of them) and starting again. This, as you can imagine, is a very expensive option.

Who Are Your Internal Stakeholders?

Your internal stakeholders are people or organizations that have a direct interest in your business. They are "insiders" by virtue of their relationships with you. They are not clients or customers, although they could be *in addition* to being internal stakeholders. They have a vested interest in seeing you succeed.

So, who then will you classify as internal stakeholders?

They include:

- Team members
- Shareholders
- Directors
- Contractors
- Subcontractors
- Suppliers
- Your franchisor
- Your franchisees
- Affiliates

There could be more, depending on your situation. Make a note of those that apply to your business by putting names next to the categories. Then jot down next to each the weighting you'd give as an internal stakeholder. Some, like team members and franchisees, will rate 100 percent, while others, like shareholders, directors, and your franchisor may rate 100 percent depending on whether they have any other interests or relationships. Contractors and subcontractors too may rate 100 percent. Others may only be rated at 10 percent or 20 percent.

Going through this exercise will reveal an interesting relationships graph that you can use to tailor your communication effort. It will also help you to ensure that you aren't leaving anyone out of the communication loop.

Internal Communication

Communication is the lifeblood of any company. And just as healthy blood needs to flow through clear, open veins, so too must a company have a policy of open communication channels for healthy communication to exist.

Furthermore, in order to facilitate effective communications, a good, trusting, and nonthreatening relationship must exist between all parties.

What exactly is effective communication, then?

Effective communication exists when the sender of a message receives sufficient feedback from the recipient of that message to indicate that the contents of the message was fully received and understood. Or to put it another way, effective communication is the result you get. If you're not getting the response you want, you're not communicating correctly. Get it?

Internal communication is such an important area for business that it has become a specialist area in its own right. It is now recognized that good internal relations lead to good internal communications, which in turn results in reduced internal conflict, increased harmony, and a greater understanding of the goals that need to be achieved. Get this right and you are well on your way to creating a successful business.

Internal communication occurs within a system, whereas external communication occurs between external systems. I have used the word system here in preference to organization because some internal stakeholders might actually belong to another business but be considered internal stakeholders by virtue of their interest in the business. Internal communication also exists on various levels: the interpersonal level, the intragroup level, and the intraorganizational level.

What is the purpose of internal communications? Why is it so important? Why can't we just communicate as and when we need to?

Internal communication basically has four main functions, which are:

- To manage information.

- To manage the identification of problems and solutions.

- To manage conflict.

- To manage and regulate behavior.

As you can see, it covers a wide range of important areas. Get your internal communication wrong and you can expect problems on a wide front, but get it right and you'll join an exclusive group of companies that enjoys fantastic working relationships with all their stakeholders. Internal harmony leads to greatly increased productivity and efficiency, which, in turn, will manifest itself on your bottom line.

Understanding Human Behavior

The way organizations communicate is so important. It affects not only their ability to promote themselves and get potential customers to take notice and consider them when needing to buy something, it also affects their ability to actually convert these prospects into actual customers. Once that is done, the way the business communicates further with their customers will dictate whether they buy from them again or increase the amount of money they spend.

Of course, an organization's ability to communicate also influences the morale of its team members and other stakeholders. Disgruntled team members aren't likely to "go the extra mile" for any business and as a result, that little bit of extra profit that could have been made from a transaction will slip you by.

Most large corporations understand the need for good communication in general and even better internal communication in particular. That's why they have whole departments assigned to look after it. They have Public Relations Departments, Communication Departments, Consumer Relations Departments, Internal Affairs Departments, and Corporate Communications Departments. But what of small businesses? How many of them spend any time on this vital subject? How many claim they can't afford the luxury?

Luxury? It's a necessity. You see, they should really be saying that the one thing they can't afford is to go broke.

Understand that, in order to make internal communication one of your strengths and not weaknesses, you don't need to create a whole department that will be staffed by experts. It can be handled on a very basic level, because it is really only basic human behavior. Get in the habit of communicating openly with all your internal stakeholders and make open communication part of your company's culture. Get everyone involved. Take away their fear of "opening themselves up" by ensuring that there are no recriminations for being open and honest.

The first thing you need to do to accomplish this is to understand as much as you can about human behavior.

Human behavior can be approached from two basic viewpoints: the psychological and the social. These two approaches are not new; they go back to the ancient Greeks. Aristotle emphasized the individual and Plato favored understanding human behavior by studying social relations. Then, in the nineteenth century, a new approach came into fashion when the philosopher August Compte proposed a mix of the two approaches. He favored studying both individual and social behavior.

All three approaches are useful when it comes to understanding how people behave in organizations. The psychological perspective looks at how individuals affect others and how they affect the organization. The sociological perspective looks at how organizations affect the behavior of individual people, and the integrative perspective looks at how both organizations and individuals interact with each other.

Let's take a quick look at these different approaches as a means of highlighting some of the factors you need to consider when designing your communication processes.

Psychological Approach

The types of variables that affect the way individuals communicate include the way they see themselves in their work situation, their level of reluctance to communicate, and their level of satisfaction when communicating. People continue working for an organization just as long as it meets their individual needs.

Sociological Approach

The organization's social structure, the relationships they have with the group, the amount of influence they enjoy, and the communication networks they belong to affect their communication behavior. This approach maintains that the way people behave is determined by the limits placed on them by the organization, or society in general. The social environment in which they live determines their behavior.

Integrative Approach

This approach says that people communicate for two basic reasons: they have a *need* to do so and they are *required* to do so. This approach is probably closer to the mark for most businesses.

There is a relationship between people's own individual behavior patterns and that expected of them by the companies they work for. The real question business owners need to ask themselves is whether their internal communication policies are correctly balanced so that both the psychological and the social factors that affect the way people behave, and therefore communicate, are sufficiently catered to.

The next question business owners need to ask themselves is whether they are providing the right psychological conditions within their businesses for team members to thrive and flourish. What are these conditions and how do you know if you are meeting them? You need to think about the following:

- Are your team members versatile in the roles they fill? Can they do more than one job?

- Are your team members involved in their jobs? Are they just going through the motions or really taking ownership of their jobs?

- How much time do they spend doing their work?

- How comfortable are your team members in performing their jobs?

- Are your team members skilled enough to carry out their tasks?

Get this right and you'll have a team that derives a great amount of job satisfaction from coming to work each day. Not only that, but they'll ensure your business functions as efficiently and profitably as possible. You'll be creating an environment of trust that will ultimately allow you to spend less time working *in* the business supervising others and more time working *on* the business, planning future directions, strategies, and growth.

Types of Communication Models

There are horses for courses, as the old saying goes. The same applies to communicating in business. It should be apparent that there is no single communication model that should be used in any business. Businesses are all different; they have different cultures, functions, and histories. They also operate in vastly different environments and require different management styles to survive. A company that is merging with another requires a completely different management style to one that is ticking along just nicely.

Generally speaking, most organizations fall into one of two broad categories: autocratic and democratic. They can also be categorized according to whether they focus primarily on work-oriented roles or people-oriented roles. Some could be a mixture of all four and would be thought of as being balanced.

Depending on what basic design the organization has, a suitable communication strategy would be adopted to match. Let's look at these in a little more detail.

Work-Oriented Organizations

A large factory would be classed as a work-oriented business. Here the communication style would focus on job-related matters far more than personal issues. Managers would be more interested in whether team members were meeting production quotas than on how they were doing in their social or family lives. Relationships would tend to be more formal and structured, and this would be reflected in the behavior of team members at work. Internal communications would also reflect this.

Person-Oriented Organizations

A consulting business would be far more people oriented than work oriented and would place more emphasis on people than tasks. The overriding impression would be of a friendly, warm business where everyone gets along really well together. Now this might not be true, but it would be the impression an outsider got when dealing with the business. Internal communications would be far more personal and team members would be encouraged to have their say and be respected for it. People's needs are given a higher priority here than work.

Balanced Organizations

Family businesses are typical balanced organizations. Here family members intersperse family and business topics all the time.

Autocratic Organizations

The army is a good example of an autocratic organization. They tend to be hierarchical in structure, with the different jobs being based on specialized functions.

Democratic Organizations

In these organizations, team members share their roles. They can be family businesses, small businesses, or even larger progressive companies.

It's important to remember that, once you have determined which category your business falls into, you need to ensure that your communication style suits. And remember too that one communication style is not better than the others; they suit different situations. The important thing is to ensure you don't have a mismatch in your business.

Franchise Relationships—A Special Case

In the franchise industry, the question of relationships plays a very important, and prominent, role in the success of any franchise system. Relationships are vitally important.

These are some special considerations to bear in mind that don't apply to other types of business. You see, a franchise involves a very special type of relationship between the franchisor and the franchisee. This relationship is far more complicated than is the case with other businesses because it is a complex one, being both a business relationship and, at the same time, a legal one.

Apart from all the usual considerations that apply to internal and external relationships, you need to overlay them with the special considerations that apply to franchises. Pay attention to them and you'll be well on your way to running a successful franchise operation.

So, here then are those special considerations.

1. Keep your relationship with your franchisor (or franchisees) cordial. The nature of the franchise method of doing business means you will get close to your franchisor (or franchisees) and there is a very strong temptation to develop friendships. This is often the case the longer you are in business. Avoid this, as there will come times when disagreements will arise and you could have to resort to mediation. Also, friendships can become abused to get your wish across. "Oh come on, John, don't worry about it. It is going to be just fine. Remember last year when sales were down and I missed two royalty payments in a row? I came good then, didn't I?" Taking advantage of a friendship is one of the most dangerous things you can do as a business owner. Fallouts will be even nastier and more traumatic than if your relationship were on a more cordial and businesslike footing. Recovery is far quicker after a business dispute, and individuals tend not to get drawn into uncompromising situations. After all, business is business.

2. Don't procrastinate. Make decisions quickly and firmly. Remember, the buck really does stop with you. Avoid the temptation to flick any challenge to your franchisor (or to pass it down to your franchisees).

3. Business must be fun, so open up your communication channels. Work on balancing your business, private, and spiritual lives. Don't let your business life dominate, as this is the quickest way to destroy the other two.

4. Try new things. Don't stagnate. The franchise business must be dynamic to survive. What works today might not work tomorrow. If you try

something new and it produces fantastic results, let others in your system know. If you're a franchisee, pass this information on to your franchisor, who might want to incorporate it in the system for the benefit of others. If you are a franchisor, then actively try new things so your franchises can remain at the cutting edge of their industry. Constantly give them new ammunition, and they'll love you forever.

5. Be willing to listen and learn. Don't think you have all the answers. Business is a two-way street and we all can learn new things every day if only we wanted to. Knowledge is, after all, one of your best weapons.

6. Abide by the system. Do what the system requires you, as a franchisee, to do. Remember that it has been tried and tested. And remember too that business is very similar to baking; if you want to bake a chocolate cake, all you have to do is follow the recipe and you'll end up with the chocolate cake. But deviate or leave out a few ingredients and you'll end up with a very different result. Remember, when you buy a franchise, you are buying a system, so use it. Why buy otherwise? You'd be better off starting your own business from scratch if that were the case.

7. Learn to ask for help. Battling on just because you are too proud to ask for assistance will get you nowhere. All you may achieve (apart from failure) is the wrath of your franchisor.

8. Focus on your own success and not finding fault with your franchisor. That will get you nowhere and make you no friends. Don't become one of those noisy people who finds fault with everything. That's being a *victim* and not a *victor*. It's avoiding responsibility and blaming others for your own shortcomings. You will be falling into the trap of digging your own grave. You will become the victim of the self-fulfilling prophecy.

"One of the keys to success in franchising is
to carefully select your franchisees."

Brad Sugars

■ Conclusion

Now you have all the keys to enable you to successfully enter the wonderful world of franchising. Whether your interest is in becoming a franchisee, a franchisor, or a seller of a franchise, you should know enough now to avoid many of the pitfalls others fall into.

You'll have a few other advantages too, like understanding the franchise industry and what makes it tick. You'll have a very good understanding too of how the industry came about, its importance in today's global and local economy, and where it's heading.

But that's not all you will have gained from reading this book. You will have learned firsthand from me all about the mind-set you'll need to succeed. You see, it's really all about attitude. You need to have the right attitude, or frame of mind, to win at this game. You need to understand the need to have fun while you're doing it and you need to understand all about relationships and human behavior.

By taking a closer look at what others have found, by hearing their stories as told by them, and by learning from my experiences, you'll not only dramatically improve your chances of succeeding in whatever you're doing in franchising, but you'll also be avoiding the trap of reinventing the wheel. Understand that business is just a game, and games have rules and a referee. Obey the rules and you won't receive penalties. Obey the rules and you'll get along with the referee. Break them and you'll have the ref watching you closely, ready to whistle. Players have to know and understand the rules of the game before they take to the field. They also have to develop a good working relationship with the ref and to respect any decision the ref makes.

Business in general, and franchising in particular, is just the same. Your franchise system is the game, you are the player, and your franchisor is the referee. You could also be the ref, if you are a franchisor, of course. But you get my point.

Succeeding in franchising is as simple as that. Understand the rules and the importance of sticking to the rules and working on developing and maintaining a good relationship with those in your system, and you'll immediately find yourself so far ahead of the pack it won't be funny. Then all you need to do is to play the game—or follow the system.

Now it's up to you. You have the keys; all you have to do is to decide whether to use them.

▌ Getting into *Action*

So, when is the best time to start?

Now—right now—so let me give you a step-by-step method to get yourself onto the same success path of many of my clients and the clients of my team at *Action International.*

Start testing and measuring now.

You'll want to ask your customers and prospects how they found out about you and your business. This will give you an idea of what's been working and what hasn't. You also want to concentrate on the five areas of the business chassis. Remember:

1. Number of Leads from each campaign.
2. Conversion Rate from each and every campaign.
3. Number of Transactions on average per year per customer.
4. Average Dollar Sale from each campaign.
5. Your Margins on each product or service.

The Number of Leads is easy; just take a measure for four weeks, average it out, and multiply by 50 working weeks of the year. Of course you'd ask each lead where they came from so you've got enough information to make advertising decisions.

The Conversion Rate is a little trickier, not because it's hard to measure, but because we want to know a few more details. You want to know what level of conversion you have from each and every type of marketing strategy you use. Remember that some customers won't buy right away, so keep accurate records on each and every lead.

To find the Number of Transactions you'll need to go through your records. Hopefully you can find the transaction history of at least 50 of your past customers and then average out their yearly purchases.

The Average Dollar Sale is as simple as it sounds. The total dollars sold divided by the number of sales. The best information you can collect is the average from each marketing campaign you run, so that you know where the real profit is coming from.

And, of course, your margins. An Average Margin is good to know and measure, but to know the margins on everything you sell is the most powerful knowledge you can collect.

If you're having any challenges with your testing and measuring, be sure to contact your nearest *Action International* Business Coach. She'll be able to help you through and show you the specialized documents to use.

If, by chance, you're thinking of racing ahead before you test and measure, remember this. It's impossible to improve a score when you don't know what the score is.

So you've got your starting point. You know exactly what's going on in your business right now. In fact, you know more about not only what's happening right now, but also the factors that are going to create what will happen tomorrow.

The next step in your business growth is simple.

Let's decide what you want out of the business—in other words, your goals. Here are the main points I want you to plan for.

How many hours do you want to work each week? How much money do you want to take out of the business each month? And, most importantly, when do you want to finish the business?

By "finish" the business, I mean when it will be systematized enough so it can run without your having to be there. Remember this about business; a little bit of planning goes a long way, but to make a plan you have to have a destination.

Once again, if you're having difficulty, talk to an *Action International* Business Coach. He'll know exactly how to help you find what it is you really want out of both your business and your life.

Now the real work begins.

Remember, our goal is to get a 10 percent increase in each area over the next 12 months. Choose well, but I want to warn you of one thing, one thing I can literally guarantee.

Eight out of 10 marketing campaigns you run *will not work.*

That's why when you choose to run, say, an advertising campaign in your local newspaper, you've got to run at least 10 different ads. When you select a direct mail campaign, you should send out at least 10 different letters to test, and so on.

Make sure you get at least five strategies under each heading and plan to run at least one, preferably two, at least each month for the next 12 months.

Don't work on just one of the five areas at a time; mix it up a little so you get the synergy of all five areas working together.

Now, this is the most important advice I can give you:

Learn how to make each and every strategy work. Don't just think you know what to do; go through my hints and tips, read more books, listen to as many tapes as you can, watch all the videos you can find, talk to the experts, and make sure you get the most advantage you can before you invest a whole lot of money.

The next 12 months are going to be a matter of doing the numbers, running the campaigns, testing headlines, testing offers, testing prices, and, of course, measuring the results.

By the end of it you should have at least five new strategies in each of the five areas working together to produce a great result.

Once again I want to stress that this will work and this will make your business grow as long as *you* work it.

Is it simple? *Yes.*

Is it easy? *No.*

You'll have to work hard. If you can get the guidance of someone who's been there before you, then get it.

Whatever you do, start it now, start it today, and most importantly, make the most of every day. Your past does not equal your future; you decide your future right here and right now.

Be who you want to be, *do* what you need to do, in order to *have* what you want to have.

Positive *thought* without positive *Action* leaves you with positively *nothing*. I called my company *Action International,* not Theory International, or Yeah, I read that book International, but *Action International.*

So take the first step—and get into *Action.*

■ ABOUT THE AUTHOR

Bradley J. Sugars

Brad Sugars is a world-renowned Australian entrepreneur, author, and business coach who has helped more than a million clients around the world find business and personal success.

He's a trained accountant, but as he puts it, most of his experience comes from owning his own companies. Brad's been in business for himself since age 15 in some way or another, although his father would argue he started at 7 when he was caught selling his Christmas presents to his brothers. He's owned and operated more than two dozen companies, from pizza to ladies fashion, from real estate to insurance and many more.

His main company, *Action International*, started from humble beginnings in the back bedroom of a suburban home in 1993 when Brad started teaching business owners how to grow their sales and marketing results. Now *Action* has nearly 1000 franchises in 19 countries and is ranked in the top 100 franchises in the world.

Brad Sugars has spoken on stage with the likes of Tom Hopkins, Brian Tracy, John Maxwell, Robert Kiyosaki, and Allen Pease, written books with people like Anthony Robbins, Jim Rohn, and Mark Victor Hansen, appeared on countless TV and radio programs and in literally hundreds of print articles around the globe. He's been voted as one of the Most Admired Entrepreneurs by the readers of *E-Spy* magazine—next to the likes of Rupert Murdoch, Henry Ford, Richard Branson, and Anita Roddick.

Today, *Action International* has coaches across the globe and is ranked as one of the Top 25 Fastest Growing Franchises on the planet as well as the #1 Business Consulting Franchise. The success of *Action International* is simply attributed to the fact that they apply the strategies their coaches use with business owners.

Brad is a proud father and husband, the chairman of a major children's charity, and in his own words, "a very average golfer."

Check out Brad's Web site www.bradsugars.com and read the literally hundreds of testimonials from those who've gone before you.

▐ RECOMMENDED READING LIST

ACTION INTERNATIONAL BOOK LIST

"The only difference between *you* now and *you* in 5 years' time will be the people you meet and the books you read." Charlie Tremendous Jones

"And, the only difference between *your* income now and *your* income in 5 years' time will be the people you meet, the books you read, the tapes you listen to, and then how *you* apply it all." Brad Sugars

- *The E-Myth Revisited* by Michael E. Gerber
- *My Life in Advertising & Scientific Advertising* by Claude Hopkins
- *Tested Advertising Methods* by John Caples
- *Building the Happiness Centered Business* by Dr. Paddi Lund
- *Write Language* by Paul Dunn & Alan Pease
- *7 Habits of Highly Effective People* by Steven Covey
- *First Things First* by Steven Covey
- *Awaken the Giant Within* by Anthony Robbins
- *Unlimited Power* by Anthony Robbins
- *22 Immutable Laws of Marketing* by Al Ries & Jack Trout
- *21 Ways to Build a Referral Based Business* by Brad Sugars
- *21 Ways to Increase Your Advertising Response* by Mark Tier
- *The One Minute Salesperson* by Spencer Johnson & Larry Wilson
- *The One Minute Manager* by Spencer Johnson & Kenneth Blanchard
- *The Great Sales Book* by Jack Collis
- *Way of the Peaceful Warrior* by Dan Millman
- *How to Build a Championship Team*—Six Audio tapes by Blair Singer
- Brad Sugars "Introduction to Sales & Marketing" 3-hour Video
- Leverage—Board Game by Brad Sugars
- *17 Ways to Increase Your Business Profits* booklet & tape by Brad Sugars. FREE OF CHARGE to Business Owners

*To order Brad Sugars' products from the recommended reading list, call your nearest *Action International* office today.

■ The 18 Most Asked Questions about Working with an *Action International* Business Coach

And 18 great reasons why you'll jump at the chance to get your business flying and make your dreams come true

1. So who is *Action International?*

Action International is a business Coaching and Consulting company started in 1993 by entrepreneur and author Brad Sugars. With offices around the globe and business coaches from Singapore to Sydney to San Francisco, *Action International* has been set up with you, the business owner, in mind.

Unlike traditional consulting firms, *Action* is designed to give you both short-term assistance and long-term training through its affordable Mentoring approach. After 12 years teaching business owners how to succeed, *Action's* more than 10,000 clients and 1,000,000 seminar attendees will attest to the power of the programs.

Based on the sales, marketing, and business management systems created by Brad Sugars, your *Action* Coach is trained to not only show you how to increase your business revenues and profits, but also how to develop the business so that you as the owner work less and relax more.

Action International is a franchised company, so your local *Action* Coach is a fellow business owner who's invested her own time, money, and energy to make her business succeed. At *Action,* your success truly does determine our success.

2. And, why do I need a Business Coach?

Every great sports star, business person, and superstar is surrounded by coaches and advisors.

And, as the world of business moves faster and gets more competitive, it's difficult to keep up with both the changes in your industry and the innovations in sales, marketing, and management strategies. Having a business coach is no longer a luxury; it's become a necessity.

On top of all that, it's impossible to get an objective answer from yourself. Don't get me wrong. You can survive in business without the help of a Coach, but it's almost impossible to thrive.

A Coach *can* see the forest for the trees. A Coach will make you focus on the game. A Coach will make you run more laps than you feel like. A Coach will tell it like it is. A Coach will give you small pointers. A Coach will listen. A Coach will be your marketing manager, your sales director, your training coordinator, your partner, your confidant, your mentor, your best friend, and an *Action* Business Coach will help you make your dreams come true.

3. Then, what's an Alignment Consultation?

Great question. It's where an *Action* Coach starts with every business owner. You'll invest a minimum of $1295, and during the initial 2 to 3 hours your Coach invests with you, he'll learn as much as he can about your business, your goals, your challenges, your sales, your marketing, your finances, and so much more.

All with three goals in mind: To know exactly where your business is now. To clarify your goals both in the business and personally. And thirdly, to get the crucial pieces of information he needs to create your businesses *Action* Plan for the next 12 months.

Not a traditional business or marketing plan mind you, but a step-by-step plan of *Action* that you'll work through as you continue with the Mentor Program.

4. So, what, then, is the Mentor Program?

Simply put, it's where your *Action* Coach will work with you for a full 12 months to make your goals a reality. From weekly coaching calls and goal-setting sessions, to creating marketing pieces together, you will develop new sales strategies and business systems so you can work less and learn all that you need to know about how to make your dreams come true.

You'll invest between $995 and $10,000 a month and your Coach will dedicate a minimum of 5 hours a month to working with you on your sales, marketing, team building, business development, and every step of the *Action* Plan you created from your Alignment Consultation.

Unlike most consultants, your *Action* Coach will do more than just show you what to do. She'll be with you when you need her most, as each idea takes shape, as each campaign is put into place, as you need the little pointers on making it happen, when you need someone to talk to, when you're faced with challenges and, most importantly, when you're just not sure what to do next. Your Coach will be there every step of the way.

5. Why at least 12 months?

If you've been in business for more than a few weeks, you've seen at least one or two so called "quick fixes."

Most Consultants seem to think they can solve all your problems in a few hours or a few days. At *Action* we believe that long-term success means not just scraping the surface and doing it for you. It means doing it with you, showing you how to do it, working alongside you, and creating the success together.

Over the 12 months, you'll work on different areas of your business, and month by month you'll not only see your goals become a reality, you'll gain both the confidence and the knowledge to make it happen again and again, even when your first 12 months of Coaching is over.

6. How can you be sure this will work in my industry and in my business?

Very simple. You see at *Action,* we're experts in the areas of sales, marketing, business development, business management, and team building just to name a few. With 328 different profit-building strategies, you'll soon see just how powerful these systems are.

You, on the other hand, are the expert in your business and together we can apply the *Action* systems to make your business fly.

Add to this the fact that within the *Action* Team at least one of our Coaches has either worked with, managed, worked in, or even owned a business that's the same or very similar to yours. Your *Action* Coach has the full resources of the entire *Action* team to call upon for every challenge you have. Imagine hundreds of experts ready to help you.

7. Won't this just mean more work?

Of course when you set the plan with your *Action* Coach, it'll all seem like a massive amount of work, but no one ever said attaining your goals would be easy.

In the first few months, it'll take some work to adjust, some work to get over the hump so to speak. The further you are into the program, the less and less work you'll have to do.

You will, however, be literally amazed at how focused you'll be and how much you'll get done. With focus, an *Action* Coach, and most importantly the *Action* Systems, you'll be achieving a whole lot more with the same or even less work.

8. How will I find the time?

Once again the first few months will be the toughest, not because of an extra amount of work, but because of the different work. In fact, your *Action* Coach will show you how to, on a day-to-day basis, get more work done with less effort.

In other words, after the first few months you'll find that you're not working more, just working differently. Then, depending on your goals from about month six onwards, you'll start to see the results of all your work, and if you choose to, you can start working less than ever before. Just remember, it's about changing what you do with your time, *not* putting in more time.

9. How much will I need to invest?

Nothing, if you look at it from the same perspective as we do. That's the difference between a cost and an investment. Everything you do with your *Action* Coach is a true investment in your future.

Not only will you create great results in your business, but you'll end up with both an entrepreneurial education second to none, and the knowledge that you can repeat your successes over and over again.

As mentioned, you'll need to invest at least $1295 up to $5000 for the Alignment Consultation and Training Day, and then between $995 and $10,000 a month for the next 12 months of coaching.

Your Coach may also suggest several books, tapes, and videos to assist in your training, and yes, they'll add to your investment as you go. Why? Because having an *Action* Coach is just like having a marketing manager, a sales team leader, a trainer, a recruitment specialist, and corporate consultant all for half the price of a secretary.

10. Will it cost me extra to implement the strategies?

Once again, give your *Action* Coach just half an hour and he'll show you how to turn your marketing into an investment that yields sales and profits rather than just running up your expenses.

In most cases we'll actually save you money when we find the areas that aren't working for you. But yes, I'm sure you'll need to spend some money to make some money.

Yet, when you follow our simple testing and measuring systems, you'll never risk more than a few dollars on each campaign, and when we find the ones that work, we make sure you keep profiting from them time and again.

Remember, when you go the accounting way of saving costs, you can only ever add a few percent to the bottom line.

Following Brad Sugars' formula, your *Action* Coach will show you that through sales, marketing, and income growth, your possible returns are exponential.

The sky's the limit, as they say.

11. Are there any guarantees?

To put it bluntly, no. Your *Action* Coach will never promise any specific results, nor will she guarantee that any of your goals will become a reality.

You see, we're your coach. You're still the player, and it's up to you to take the field. Your Coach will push you, cajole you, help you, be there for you, and even do some things with you, but you've still got to do the work.

Only *you* can ever be truly accountable for your own success and at *Action* we know this to be a fact. We guarantee to give you the best service we can, to answer your questions promptly, and with the best available information. And, last but not least your *Action* Coach is committed to making you successful whether you like it or not.

That's right, once we've set the goals and made the plan, we'll do whatever it takes to make sure you reach for that goal and strive with all your might to achieve all that you desire.

Of course we'll be sure to keep you as balanced in your life as we can. We'll make sure you never compromise either the long-term health and success of your company or yourself, and more importantly your personal set of values and what's important to you.

12. What results have other business owners seen?

Anything from previously working 60 hours a week down to working just 10—right through to increases in revenues of 100s and even 1000s of percent. Results speak for themselves. Be sure to keep reading for specific examples of real people, with real businesses, getting real results.

There are three reasons why this will work for you in your business. Firstly, your *Action* Coach will help you get 100 percent focused on your goals and the step-by-step processes to get you there. This focus alone is amazing in its effect on you and your business results.

Secondly, your coach will hold you accountable to get things done, not just for the day-to-day running of the business, but for the dynamic growth of the business. You're investing in your success and we're going to get you there.

Thirdly, your Coach is going to teach you one-on-one as many of *Action's* 328 profit-building strategies as you need. So whether your goal is to be making more money, or working fewer hours or both inside the next 12 months your goals can become a reality. Just ask any of the thousands of existing *Action* clients, or more specifically, check out the results of 19 of our most recent clients shown later in this section.

13. What areas will you coach me in?

There are five main areas your *Action* Coach will work on with you. Of course, how much of each depends on you, your business, and your goals.

Sales. The backbone of creating a superprofitable business, and one area we'll help you get spectacular results in.

Marketing and Advertising. If you want to get a sale, you've got to get a prospect. Over the next 12 months your *Action* Coach will teach you Brad Sugars' amazingly simple streetwise marketing—marketing that makes profits.

Team Building and Recruitment. You'll never *wish* for the right people again. You'll have motivated and passionate team members when your Coach shows you how.

Systems and Business Development. Stop the business from running you and start running your business. Your Coach will show you the secrets to having the business work, even when you're not there.

Customer Service. How to deliver consistently, make it easy to buy, and leave your customers feeling delighted with your service. Both referrals and repeat business are centered in the strategies your Coach will teach you.

14. Can you also train my people?

Yes. We believe that training your people is almost as important as coaching you.

Your investment starts at $1500 for your entire team, and you can decide between five very powerful in-house training programs. From "*Sales Made Simple*" for your face-to-face sales team to "*Phone Power*" for your entire team's telephone etiquette and sales ability. Then you can run the *"Raving Fans"* customer service training or the *"Total Team"* training. And finally, if you're too busy earning a living to make any real money, then you've just got to attend our *"Business Academy 101."* It will make a huge impact on your finances, business, career, family, and lifestyle. You'll be amazed at how much involvement and excitement comes out of your team with each training program.

15. Can you write ads, letters, and marketing pieces for me?

Yes. Your *Action* Coach can do it for you, he can train you to do it yourself, or we can simply critique the marketing pieces you're using right now.

If you want us to do it for you, our one-time fees start at just $1195. You'll not only get one piece; we'll design several pieces for you to take to the market and see which one performs the best. Then, if it's a critique you're after, just $349 means we'll work through your entire piece and give you feedback on what to change, how to change it, and what else you should do. Last but not least, for between $15 and $795 we can recommend a variety of books, tapes, and most importantly, Brad Sugars' Instant Success series books that'll take you step-by-step through the how-tos of creating your marketing pieces.

16. Why do you also recommend books, tapes, and videos?

Basically, to save you time and money. Take Brad Sugars' *Sales Rich* DVD or Video Series, for instance. In about 16 hours you'll learn more about business than you have in the last 12 years. It'll also mean your *Action* Coach works with you on the high-level implementation rather than the very basic teaching.

It's a very powerful way for you to speed up the coaching process and get phenomenal rather than just great results.

17. When is the best time to get started?

Yesterday. OK, seriously, right now, today, this minute, before you take another step, waste another dollar, lose another sale, work too many more hours, miss another family event, forget another special occasion.

Far too many business people wait and see. They think working harder will make it all better. Remember, what you know got you to where you are. To get to where you want to go, you've got to make some changes and most probably learn something new.

There's no time like the present to get started on your dreams and goals.

18. So how do we get started?

Well, you'd better get back in touch with your *Action* Coach. There's some very simple paperwork to sign, and then you're on your way.

You'll have to invest a few hours showing them everything about your business. Together you'll get a plan created and then the work starts. Remember, it may seem like a big job at the start, but with a Coach, you're sharing the load and together you'll achieve great things.

Here's what others say about what happened after working with an *Action* business coach

Paul and Rosemary Rose—Icontact Multimedia

"Our *Action* coach showed us several ways to help market our product. We went on to triple our client base and simultaneously tripled our profits in just seven months. It was unbelievable! Last year was our best Christmas ever. We were really able to spoil ourselves!"

S. Ford—Pride Kitchens

"In 6 months, I've gone from working more than 60 hours per week in my business to less than 20, and my conversion rate's up from 19 percent to 62 percent. I've now got some life back!"

Gary and Leanne Paper—Galea Timber Products

"We achieved our goal for the 12 months within a 6-month period with a 100 percent increase in turnover and a good increase in margins. We have already recommended and will continue to recommend this program to others."

Russell, Kevin, John, and Karen—Northern Lights Power and Distribution

"Our profit margin has increased from 8 percent to 21 percent in the last 8 months. *Action* coaching focussed us on what are our most profitable markets."

Ty Pedersen—De Vries Marketing Sydney

"After just three months of coaching, my sales team's conversion rate has grown from an average of less than 12 percent to more than 23 percent and our profits have climbed by more than 30 percent."

Hank Meerkerk and Hemi McGarvey—B.O.P. School of Welding

"Last year we started off with a profit forecast, but as soon as we got *Action* involved we decided to double our forecast. We're already well over that forecast again by two-and-a-half times on turnover, and profits are even higher. Now we run a really profitable business."

Stuart Birch—Education Personnel Limited

"One direct mail letter added $40,000 to my bottom line, and working with *Action* has given me quality time to work on my business and spend time with my family."

Mark West—Wests Pumping and Irrigation

"In four months two simple strategies have increased our business more than 20 percent. We're so busy, we've had to delay expanding the business while we catch up!"

Michael Griffiths—Gym Owner

"I went from working 70 hours per week *in* the business to just 25 hours, with the rest of the time spent working *on* the business."

Cheryl Standring—In Harmony Landscapes

"We tried our own direct mail and only got a 1 percent response. With *Action* our response rate increased to 20 percent. It's definitely worth every dollar we've invested."

Jason and Chris Houston—Empradoor Finishing

"After 11 months of working with *Action,* we have increased our sales by 497 percent, and the team is working without our having to be there."

Michael Avery—Coomera Pet Motels

"I was skeptical at first, but I knew we needed major changes in our business. In 2 months, our extra profits were easily covering our investment and our predictions for the next 10 months are amazing."

Garry Norris—North Tax & Accounting

"As an accountant, my training enables me to help other business people make more money. It is therefore refreshing when someone else can help me do the same. I have a policy of only referring my clients to people who are professional, good at what they do, and who have personally given me great service. *Action* fits all three of these criteria, and I recommend *Action* to my business clients who want to grow and develop their businesses further."

Lisa Davis and Steve Groves—Mt. Eden Motorcycles

"With *Action* we increased our database from 800 to 1200 in 3 months. We consistently get about 20 new qualified people on our database each week for less than $10 per week."

Christine Pryor—U-Name-It Embroidery

"Sales for August this year have increased 352 percent. We're now targeting a different market and we're a lot more confident about what we're doing."

Joseph Saitta and Michelle Fisher—Banyule Electrics

"Working with *Action,* our inquiry rate has doubled. In four months our business has changed so much our customers love us. It's a better place for people to work and our margins are widening."

Kevin and Alison Snook—Property Sales

"In the 12 months previous to working with *Action,* we had sold one home in our subdivision. In the first eight months of working with *Action,* we sold six homes. The results speak for themselves."

Wayne Manson—Hospital Supplies

"When I first looked at the Mentoring Program it looked expensive, but from the inside looking out, its been the best money I have ever spent. Sales are up more than $3000 per month since I started, and the things I have learned and expect to learn will ensure that I will enjoy strong sustainable growth in the future."

▎ *Action* Contact Details

Action International Asia Pacific

Ground Floor, *Action* House, 2 Mayneview Street, Milton QLD 4064

Ph: +61 (0) 7 3368 2525

Fax: +61 (0) 7 3368 2535

Free Call: 1800 670 335

Action International Europe

Olympic House, Harbor Road, Howth, Co. Dublin, Ireland

Ph: +353 (0) 1-832 0213

Fax: +353 (0) 1-839 4934

Action International North America

5670 Wynn Road Suite A & C, Las Vegas, Nevada 89118

Ph: +1 (702) 795 3188

Fax: +1 (702) 795 3183

Free Call: (888) 483 2828

Action International UK

3–5 Richmond Hill, Richmond, Surrey, TW 106RE

Ph: +44 020 8948 5151

Fax: +44 020 8948 4111

Action Offices around the globe:

Australia | Canada | China | England | France | Germany | Hong Kong

India | Indonesia | Ireland | Malaysia | Mexico | New Zealand

Phillippines | Scotland | Spain | Singapore | USA | Wales

Here's how you can profit from all of Brad's ideas with your local *Action* International **Business Coach**

Just like a sporting coach pushes an athlete to achieve optimum performance, provides them with support when they are exhausted, and teaches the athlete to execute plays that the competition does not anticipate.

A business coach will make you run more laps than you feel like. A business coach will show it like it is. And a business coach will listen.

The role of an *Action* Business Coach is to show you how to improve your business through guidance, support, and encouragement. Your coach will help you with your sales, marketing, management, team building, and so much more. Just like a sporting coach, your *Action* Business Coach will help you and your business perform at levels you never thought possible.

Whether you've been in business for a week or 20 years, it's the right time to meet with and see how you'll profit from an *Action* Coach.

As the owner of a business it's hard enough to keep pace with all the changes and innovations going on in your industry, let alone to find the time to devote to sales, marketing, systems, planning and team management, and then to run your business as well.

As the world of business moves faster and becomes more competitive, having a Business Coach is no longer a luxury; it has become a necessity. Based on the sales, marketing, and business management systems created by Brad Sugars, your *Action* Coach is trained to not only show you how to increase your business revenues and profits but also how to develop your business so that you, as the owner, can take back control. All with the aim of your working less and relaxing more. Making money is one thing; having the time to enjoy it is another.

Your *Action* Business Coach will become your marketing manager, your sales director, your training coordinator, your confidant, your mentor. In short, your *Action* Coach will help you make your business dreams come true.

ATTENTION BUSINESS OWNERS
You can increase your profits now

Here's how you can have one of Brad's *Action* *International* Business Coaches guide you to success.

Like every successful sporting icon or team, a business needs a coach to help it achieve its full potential. In order to guarantee your business success, you can have one of Brad's team as your business coach. You will learn about how you can get amazing results with the help of the team at *Action* *International*.

The business coaches are ready to take you and your business on a journey that will reward you for the rest of your life. You see, we believe *Action* speaks louder than words.

Complete and post this card to your local *Action* office to discover how our team can help you increase your income today!

Action International

The World's Number-1 Business Coaching Team

Name ....

Position ....

Company ....

Address ....

....

Country ....

Phone ....

Fax ....

Email ....

Referred by ....

How do I become an *Action* International **Business Coach?**

If you choose to invest your time and money in a great business and you're looking for a white-collar franchise opportunity to build yourself a lifestyle, an income, a way to take control of your life and, a way to get great personal satisfaction …

Then you've just found the world's best team!

Now, it's about finding out if you've got what it takes to really enjoy and thrive in this amazing business opportunity.

Here are the 4 things we look for in every *Action* Coach:

1. You've got to love succeeding

We're looking for people who love success, who love getting out there and making things happen. People who enjoy mixing with other people, people who thrive on learning and growing, and people who want to charge an hourly rate most professionals only dream of.

2. You've got to love being in charge of your own life

When you're ready to take control, the key is to be in business for yourself, but not by yourself. *Action*'s support, our training, our world leading systems, and the backup of a global team are all waiting to give you the best chance of being an amazing business success.

3. You've got to love helping people

Being a great Coach is all about helping yourself by helping others. The first time clients thank you for showing them step by step how to make more money and work less within their business, will be the day you realize just how great being an *Action* Business Coach really is.

4. You've got to love a great lifestyle

Working from home, setting your own timetable, spending time with family and friends, knowing that the hard work you do is for your own company and, not having to climb a so-called corporate ladder. This is what lifestyle is all about. Remember, business is supposed to give you a life, not take it away.

Our business is booming and we're seriously looking for people ready to find out more about how becoming a member of the *Action International* Business Coaching team is going to be the best decision you've ever made.

Apply online now at www.action-international.com

Here's how you can network, get new leads, build yourself an instant sales team, learn, grow and build a great team of supportive business owners around you by checking into your local *Action* Profit Club

Joining your local *Action* Profit Club is about more than just networking, it's also the learning and exchanging of profitable ideas.

Embark on a journey to a more profitable enterprise by meeting with fellow, like-minded business owners.

An *Action* Profit Club is an excellent way to network with business people and business owners. You will meet every two weeks for breakfast to network and learn profitable strategies to grow your business.

Here are three reasons why *Action* *International's* Profit Clubs work where other networking groups don't:

1. You know networking is a great idea. The challenge is finding the time and maintaining the motivation to keep it up and make it a part of your business. If you're not really having fun and getting the benefits, you'll find it gets easier to find excuses that stop you going. So, we guarantee you will always have fun and learn a lot from your bi-weekly group meetings.
2. The real problem is that so few people do any work 'on' their business. Instead they generally work "in" it, until it's too late. By being a member of an *Action* Profit Club, you get to attend FREE business-building workshops run by Business Coaches that teach you how to work "on" your business and avoid this common pitfall and help you to grow your business.
3. Unlike other groups, we have marketing systems to assist in your groups' growth rather than just relying on you to bring in new members. This way you can concentrate on YOUR business rather than on ours.

Latest statistics show that the average person knows at least 200 other contacts. By being a member of your local *Action* Profit Club, you have an instant network of around 3,000 people

Join your local *Action* Profit Club today.

Apply online now at www.actionprofitclub.com

LEVERAGE—The Game of Business
Your Business Success is just a Few Games Away

Leverage—The Game of Business is a fun way to learn how to succeed in business fast.

The rewards start flowing the moment you start playing!

Leverage is three hours of fun, learning, and discovering how you can be an amazingly successful business person.

It's a breakthrough in education that will have you racking up the profits in no time. The principles you take away from playing this game will set you up for a life of business success. It will open your mind to what's truly possible. Apply what you learn and **sit back and watch your profits soar.**

By playing this fun and interactive business game, you will learn:

- How to quickly raise your business income
- How business people can become rich and successful in a short space of time
- How to create a business that works without you

Isn't it time you had the edge over your competition?

Leverage has been played by all age groups from 12-85 and has been a huge learning experience for all. The most common comment we hear is: 'I thought I knew a lot, and just by playing a simple board game I have realized I have a long way to go. The knowledge I've gained from playing Leverage will make me thousands! Thanks for the lesson.'

To order your copy online today, please visit www.bradsugars.com

Also available in the

THE BUSINESS COACH

Learn how to master the six steps on
the ladder of success

(0-07-146672-X)

INSTANT REPEAT BUSINESS

Build a solid and loyal
customer base

(0-07-146666-5)

THE REAL ESTATE COACH

Invest in real estate with
little or no cash

(0-07-146662-2)

INSTANT SALES

Master the crucial first minute of
any sales call

(0-07-146664-9)

INSTANT PROMOTIONS

Create powerful press releases, amazing
ads, and brilliant brochures

(0-07-146665-7)

INSTANT SUCCESS

Real Results. Right Now.

Instant Success series.

INSTANT CASHFLOW
Turn every lead into a sale
(0-07-146659-2)

BILLIONAIRE IN TRAINING
Learn the wealth building secrets
of billionaires
(0-07-146661-4)

INSTANT PROFIT
Boost your bottom line with
a cash-building plan
(0-07-146668-1)

SUCCESSFUL FRANCHISING
Learn how to buy or sell a franchise
(0-07-146671-1)

INSTANT ADVERTISING
Create ads that stand out and sell
(0-07-146660-6)

INSTANT REFERRALS
Never cold call or chase after
customers again
(0-07-146667-3)

INSTANT LEADS
Generate a steady flow of leads
(0-07-146663-0)

INSTANT SYSTEMS
Stop running your business and start
growing it
(0-07-146670-3)

INSTANT TEAM BUILDING
Learn the six keys to a winning team
(0-07-146669-X)

*Your source for the strategies, skills,
and confidence every business owner
needs to succeed.*